DEVELOPING TEAMS
THROUGH PROJECT-BASED LEARNING

Developing Teams Through Project-Based Learning

Jean Atkinson

Gower

Published by
Gower Publishing Limited
Gower House
Croft Road
Aldershot
Hampshire GU11 3HR
England

Gower Publishing Company
131 Main Street
Burlington VT 05401-5600 USA

Jean Atkinson has asserted her right under the Copyright, Designs and Patents Act 1988 to be identified as the author of this work.

Atkinson, Jean
    Developing teams through project-based learning
    1.Teams in the workplace – Management   2.Industrial project
    management
    I.Title
    658.4'02

ISBN 0 566 08367 1

Library of Congress Cataloging-in-Publication Data

Atkinson, Jean.
    Developing teams through project-based learning / Jean Atkinson.
        p. cm.
    Includes bibliographical references.
    ISBN 0-566-08367-1 (hardback)
    1. Teams in the workplace–Management. 2. Industrial project management.
    I. Title.

HD66.A85 2001
658.4'02–dc21

                                                                00-069173

Typeset in Palatino by Manton Typesetters, Louth, Lincolnshire, UK and printed in Great Britain by TJ International Ltd, Padstow, Cornwall

Contents

List of figures

Preface

This is not another book on project management, although inevitably we shall be following a project through as we go, with ideas to help you bring it in on time, to required quality and within budget. Neither is it simply another book on team-building. This is primarily a book about the people involved in the project, and how you can use your project as a vehicle for developing those individuals into a team.

In some cases you will be leading a team which has been specially put together to carry out a project. People will have been selected because of a particular skill and you may well have had the facility of choosing those people yourself. They will work on the project as their sole responsibility, and at the end of the project they will disband, go back to their original jobs, no longer be working as a team. This book, however, is about the other sort of team – the group of people who are working together all the time in the course of their normal duties but whom you, as leader, see as a group and not a team. You will be using a project as a means of welding them together into a team whose cohesion will last long after the project is completed. Inevitably, the project will be added to your normal responsibilities – you will have to maintain production, or keep up customer care, or produce sales figures, or get the invoices out on time. Therefore your project will need to fit into this regular routine – you will find some ideas in Appendix A.

I have tried to avoid as much as possible the often irritating 'him/her' expression by using the pronoun 'she' in some places and 'he' in others, thus acknowledging that both genders are in fact represented in the workforce. I hope this is acceptable to all readers.

At the end of each chapter, you will find one or more 'think-sheets' to use either to clarify your own thinking on that particular subject or to involve your team in discussion – or indeed both. These are my original and copyright work, but I am happy for you to photocopy them to use *with your own team only*. If you are your organization's training manager, you may use them with your own delegates only. If you are a freelance trainer, then I know you'll use them anyway; all I insist upon is that you give an indication of where you have taken them from, and don't pass them off without acknowledgement. To do so will be to fall foul of the law, my publisher and my dad who's a policeman. Actually, I made up the bit about my dad, but it's the only lie in this book!

Enjoy!

Acknowledgements

I am very grateful to Nick Pareas for shoring up my weak computer skills, to Brenda Joynes for help in a panic situation, to Serina Ramos for checking my maths, and to Maureen Rose who proof-read the entire manuscript. If, despite all this help, mistakes have slipped through, these are my own.

1 Why use project-based learning?

The objectives of this chapter are:

1 To help you to identify the stage of teamwork which currently exists in your team.
2 To explain why project-based learning is effective for developing teamwork.
3 To examine examples of projects which have been used to develop teamwork.

I yield to no one in my support for platform-based training; it is how I earn most of my living. However, when it comes to teamwork, talking about it and putting it into practice are two different things. Hence this book.

Here you will learn not only the theory of team-building but also how to cope with those prima donnas, optimists, pessimists, 'no-can-do's and good team players who make up the team which will bring in a project on time, to standard and within budgets.

What is a team?

If you take a group of people and put them into matching shirts and shorts, do you have a team? Patently not.

In a team, everyone knows where the goal is and how to get to it; each member knows his place in the scheme of things; a good team player is willing to allow other people credit sometimes, rather than always wanting to hog the limelight; she knows that she is valued for the skills she brings to the game; team members may not always like each other but there is mutual respect for each other's skills; similarly they may sometimes dislike the team captain intensely for the way he's driving them, but they respect the boss because he knows what he's doing and he understands their problems. In a successful team, all know that anyone who is holding the team back will be dealt with and brought up to standard; and most of all, perhaps, every member of that team wants to be on the winning side.

All this is beautiful for the manager of a sports team, who often has the pick of the sport's players and the money to reward talent; not so hot for the leader of a work-based team who must often work with the people already to hand at the time, warts and all! We shall be discussing later how to take the various skills and personalities available and motivate, threaten and lead until the game is won.

Why projects?

So why are projects such a good idea for this kind of team-building? Because to be successful, the same rules apply. The goal must be clear and reachable; there must be mutual respect; Brenda must be willing to accept that the way Brian is doing things is not necessarily wrong just because it's not how she would work; all members must know that they are valued for their own contribution; and they must be led to see themselves as a successful team of winners. This is learning which cannot be acquired from the platform.

Simply setting the goal and then turning people loose to achieve it, though, is not likely to produce the desired results. There needs to be a compromise between delegating effectively and keeping a careful watch on progress; therefore, later on, we shall look at ways of keeping track of what is happening, of solving problems and of taking decisions – sometimes to move the goal-posts, occasionally to abort the project altogether. As part of the monitoring progress we shall discuss progress meetings – often the most wasted hours in any project but potentially tremendously useful if they are well controlled and productive. Then, since management approval is often needed for the implementation of recommendations arising from a project, we'll give some guidance in report-writing and presentation skills.

What skills will you need?

Besides presentation skills, what other competencies are needed to be a good team player? Probably the most important ones are *people skills* – tolerance, willingness to help, communication, negotiation, acceptance, persuasion. Then there are *time-linked skills* – the ability to set realistic deadlines and to work to those deadlines to maximize the use of time. At least one member of the team will need *creativity* – the ability to come up with ideas; however, if too many of the team have this gift you'll never achieve deadlines because so many individuals will be trying out a better (?) way of doing things. Therefore, *self-discipline* becomes essential. Add to these *administration skills* for keeping records and you'll realize that projects are indeed excellent vehicles for team development.

It may be that you have a team already working well, and you now want to encourage even closer working. Perhaps you are just taking over a team which is new to you, and you want to ensure that you are going to be working well together. Perhaps performance results have not been too good recently, so that you want to overcome demoralization and demotivation within the team. It's important to remember that teams don't come ready-made. They are said to go through four definite stages: forming, storming, norming, performing.

Forming

At the 'forming' stage, everyone is getting to know everyone else. Even if the team is used to working together, when they are introduced to a new project they may well go back to this stage for a short while, wondering how each is going to react to the situation. Finding themselves in new roles, there may be a little caution from team members about who is going to do what, what will be expected of them and so on. The manager will need to play a leading role at this stage, answering questions, giving reassurance, very much being the leader. When, as leader, you also have to keep up your own performance in your routine job, you may find the whole thing stressful; we shall look at stress and what you can do about it in Chapter 6.

Storming

At the next stage of team development, the manager needs to be there to sort out conflicts as they arise, as the team goes through the 'storming' stage. Personalities are beginning to emerge, some people will set themselves up as experts, others may resent this. It is a sad thing that it is at this stage that projects which are taken on board half-heartedly may well fade out, as they seem to be causing more problems than they are worth. The good project manager will encourage discussion, co-operation and group decision-making to ensure that not only does the project continue as a project, but that it leads towards the goal of greater teamwork. This is also one of the few occasions when a 'because I say so' approach may be appropriate – 'this is no longer up for discussion, here's how we're going to do it'. Rather than 'We'll try it for a month and see how it's going', use 'We'll try it for a month and then see what we need to change for it to work more effectively'.

Norming

It is worth gritting your teeth at stage two, because by the time your team reaches stage three, the worst is over. This stage is known as 'norming' because it is now that team norms, or values, are being agreed. There is little point in talking about team mission statements or acceptable ground rules to a team which is still not sure of itself as a team, or in a situation where most decisions are being questioned. When your team gets to this stage, its members are used to working together and working partnerships may be formed; you will be less of a manager and more of a consultant, just making sure that the agreed values are being observed.

Performing

By the time the 'performing' stage is reached, you will be able to leave the team very much to its own devices, knowing that they have become problem-solvers, not proliferators of problems. You will need to monitor progress, and you will also need to remember that teams can go back a stage, or even two, upon occasion – for instance, if the project starts to lag behind schedule, expect some degree of return to the 'storming' stage where people are trying to find scapegoats. This is the time to remind them of agreed team values – 'we will concentrate on putting things right, not on proving someone wrong'. You will read a lot as this book progresses about the importance of the 'next-time' approach.

Some examples of projects

What sort of project might you decide on to develop this teamwork? Well, of course, it may be one that you are asked to undertake by another manager or an outside client, either of whom will become the project's sponsor. You may well find, though, that there are projects that you can devise for yourself which will achieve your objective. Here are some examples of project-based learning to give you ideas.

In one large hotel chain I work with, the restaurant manager had been thinking for some time of holding a St George's night dinner, but had wondered whether it would be profitable. She mobilized her team to do a research project – some were responsible for costing, some for planning menus, some for canvassing customers' opinions, some for planning decorations. She delegated as much as she could, while she herself held the reins, and I was thrilled to be invited to the very successful evening which was the culmination of their work.

In a large recruitment agency, another client of mine, the branch managers had long been complaining that they were not given company cars. They felt, with some justification, that since they had to do so many client visits, a car would be an appropriate addition to their package. The area managers set a project to develop analytical skills on this. One branch manager was asked to find out leasing terms; one compared running costs of several cars; all were responsible for identifying potential business within their operating areas which they were not currently getting but could be reasonably sure of getting with more visits; one was made project leader, responsible for collating all information; and all were given the task of identifying how much it would be reasonable to add to their branch target per quarter in order to cover the cost of the car and make a profit. At the end of the six weeks allowed for research, the general consensus was that they would rather continue to use their own cars than have the increased targets. The good thing, of course, was that this was *their* decision, reached as a management team, not one which had been foisted on them from above. It also highlights an important point about a project – sometimes its result will be the finding that what was envisaged is impossible or requires too much effort to be worth implementing in view of the time involved. It's important to remember that a negative conclusion to a project may in fact be very worthwhile.

One more example of a successful project, this time in a hospital. One of the theatre sisters was concerned about the number of disposable kidney-dishes which were being used. (Just in case you haven't been in hospital, kidney-dishes are dishes shaped like kidneys, not dishes to put kidneys in. I'll pass hastily on!) She drew up a very simple record-sheet, which for a month everyone who used a kidney-dish for whatever reason was required to fill in. She discovered that instead of being used to carry syringes, dressings and so on, by far the majority of the dishes were being used as handy receptacles for rubbish and then, being disposable, were going into the bin with the rubbish. At a team meeting she discussed the amount of money being wasted in this way and stressed that the dishes would in future only be used for their proper purpose. Within the next month, the use of the dishes had gone down by 40 per cent.

You will see that these were real-life projects, developing work-based skills. At the end of the hotel example, the team could talk confidently to customers, were far more cost-conscious and creativity had been encouraged; inter-departmental communication had been improved by meetings with the chef to discuss menus and with maintenance staff to identify possibilities of and difficulties with decorating schemes. In the recruitment agency, the branch managers had learnt that there's no such thing as a free lunch – particularly in sales – and as a result of the way they had had to work together on this project they decided that they would meet as a management team on a quarterly basis to promote inter-branch business and boost their own morale. In the hospital scenario, the theatre team had developed an awareness of cost and an accountability for savings.

These are very good instances of how the clear and very real objectives of the exercises were used to develop teamwork. Certainly any competent trainer could have given platform-based guidance on the topics of customer care, strategy planning, budgeting, communication and analysis; however, it would not have had half the impact of actually using these skills in a way which necessitated maximum effort from all members to achieve success. An important part of all of these projects was the follow-up meeting afterwards, when the questions were posed: 'What have we learnt? How can we use this learning in other applications?'

As mentioned in the introduction, to talk about developing *teamwork* through projects rather suggests a team of people which is already working together and which will stay together when the project is over. When a group of specialists is brought together specifically for the life of the project, the emphasis is likely to be on the project itself and perhaps on developing individuals rather than on developing teamwork. The 'people' side of the project may be important, but the very fact that they are specialists means that each will tend to focus on his/her own part and the knowledge that the team will be disbanded at the end inevitably changes the dynamics. In the next chapter, therefore, we shall look at how we can use the dynamics created by individual personalities to produce not only an effective end to a project, but a motivated team.

Think-sheets

Before deciding how you want your people to change to become a team, it's important to identify the skills you will need to complete the project, and then identify the skills you currently have on board. The first two 'think-sheets' (which can be identified by the symbol in the top corner) are designed to help you do this. There may be a learning situation for you as leader in the 'Current Skills Mix' sheet – how well do you know your people and their capabilities, strengths and weaknesses? Can you put a name beside each skill mentioned?

You will find the sheet headed 'Our Current Team' useful for discussion at team meetings. You may well be surprised at how different individuals view the team differently. Ask 'Are we satisfied with what we've identified? Do we want to improve anything? Where shall we start? How shall we start?'

The sheets will help you confirm in your own mind the very important fact that, as we shall discuss in Chapter 2, projects mean people.

Points to consider

1 What skills shall we need between us?

2 What skills do we currently lack?

3 How can we develop these?

4 Am I, as leader, sure of what I want to achieve?

5 What will success look like?

Our current skills mix

In our team, between us we currently have some:

People who are good at analysing objectively

People who are strong on meeting deadlines

People who are good communicators

People who are good at administration

'Ideas' people

People who work well with other people

Good listeners

People who can do as they are told

Our current team

In our current team we:

	Always	Usually	Rarely	Never	Most People
Have respect for the leader					
Show respect to each other					
All have up-to-date job descriptions					
Know our importance to the company's success					
Listen to each other					
Are willing to contribute ideas					
Will go 'the extra mile'					
Are possibility thinkers					
Adapt well to change					
Meet our targets					
Are budget-conscious					
Meet deadlines					
Solve problems creatively					
Solve problems practically					
Hold effective meetings					
Compromise over disagreements					
'Bury' conflicts once they are settled					
Accept decisions without rancour					
Discuss each other's suggestions					
Avoid 'bad-mouthing' the company					
Avoid doing the same to each other					
Keep our problems within the team					
Are able to settle conflicts amicably					
Share the same values					
Want to be working where we are					
Want to be doing what we do					

Reproduced from *Developing Teams Through Project-Based Learning*,
Jean Atkinson, Gower, Aldershot, 2001.

Teamwork skills I should like this project to develop are:

Possible projects to present for team consideration are:

2 Developing the people

The objectives of this chapter are:

1 To help you appreciate and work with differing personalities to progress your project.
2 To remind you of accepted theory on motivation and to give ideas on putting theory into practice.
3 To help you to motivate yourself to lead the team.

If only the world were peopled by replicas of me – or you, or you – what a wonderful place it would be! Why was it decreed that everyone should be different? It just creates difficulties – particularly to managers, and particularly to managers of projects.

In fact, of course, it's the diversity of people that makes a team successful and progressive. If the world were in fact peopled by clones of me, everyone would have wonderful ideas, love everyone else, talk constantly and never finish anything. This is not a recipe for success. It is by accepting that we are OK and so is everyone else – for what we are, not in spite of it – that we as managers can build on complementary strengths.

Personality differences

So, stand by for some psychology. Carl Jung carried out in-depth research into certain aspects of personality which make a difference to our attitudes and behaviour. I wish I'd been introduced to these at the start of my management career – it would have made me much more tolerant and I would have stopped thinking I could motivate the team; in fact, of course, you lead a team, but you have to motivate individuals. These aspects of personality are referred to as preferences, since they reflect the way we prefer to behave – they are not excuses for behaviour, since we have the ability to adopt another personality when necessary or appropriate. No preference is better than another – just different. This begins to explain why staff management is so difficult.

The aspects of personality which were examined, first by Jung and then added to by Myers and Briggs, were: the way we 'recharge our batteries'; how we gather information; how we make decisions; and the way we relate to the world about us. We shall look at each in turn. I have changed established names for a couple of these preferences – I think mine are more immediately descriptive for our purposes (of course there's nothing inflated about my ego – I just think my names are better than those of one of the world's greatest psychology names…).

Recharging your batteries

First of all, how do you recharge your batteries? Are you 'introvert' or 'extrovert'? It is important to accept that Jung uses these terms differently from the general public's interpretation.

Extroverts
We tend to think of an extrovert as being the life and soul of the party, loud, brash. In fact, the Jungian Extrovert can be quiet when necessary, can work alone if the job dictates, but if he/she is without contact with other people for too long, the battery goes flat. The Extrovert on your team who has to work alone for

any length of time, therefore, will need to find opportunities to chat with other people – by e-mail if all else fails, or a good natter at the coffee machine; this individual will not be wasting time, simply recharging batteries.

Extroverts have few secrets – 'what you sees is what you gets'. If they have a worry or a problem about the project, they will discuss it, often with more than one person. They will find it easy to bare their souls – and may regret it next day. They are useful to your team because they have no hidden corners, no secret decisions – we (!) have to be open, because of our burning need to discuss. During a project, of course, we have to accept that we are adult people who frequently have to work outside our preference; teamwork means that we respect other people's need for privacy. To keep your extroverts fully motivated, however, you will need whenever possible to allow them to work with other people. They will be the ones in the meeting who have plenty to say (not always to the point) and will often carry out 'self-censoring' of their own ideas: 'Why don't we do this – mind you, that would take a lot of time – we probably don't have enough people – no. Forget I suggested that.' This drives other people round the table into a homicidal frenzy but then, you see, we extroverts don't really know what we're thinking until we hear ourselves saying it.

Introverts
Jungian Introverts on the other hand, tend to keep all their problems to themselves, not because they are afraid to ask for help but because they see no need – they can work things out inside themselves without external reference. You will only ever know about an introvert as much as he/she is willing to share with you. They can enjoy parties, work with other people, share jokes, but because strength is drawn from inside, they must have adequate periods of time to themselves if they are not to become stressed and function less efficiently. I was recently doing a two-day management programme with fifteen managers and I became worried by the end of the first day because I was getting very little response; they were attentive, they took notes, but in group-work they had little to say to each other and although they would answer questions with yes and no, only a couple of them actually contributed fully. By the end of the day I was

quite seriously wondering if I had lost it as far as training was concerned. Imagine my relief when on the second day they did a questionnaire which showed that thirteen of them were introvert! Does this shed a different light on that colleague who never comes with you all for a drink? Or, if you are introvert, are you starting to see why your boss drives you mad by stopping for a chat every time she passes your desk?

Acquiring information

So much for the way we relate to others; now let's look at ways in which we acquire information.

Sensates (Here and Nows)

Some of us take in information through the senses, and anything which can't be registered by sight, sound, touch, taste or smell is suspect. These people live in the present tense. They don't see visions or have dreams, but are excellent in using current data to draw conclusions or show trends. They tend to use traditional problem-solving methods, not making leaps of imagination; they work happily with fine detail and their findings can be relied on. They are usually 'good company men and women', believing that 'you can't fight City Hall'. Jung's name for these is 'Sensate' – acquiring information through the senses – but in the everyday work world I prefer to call them 'Here and Nows'; and every team needs at least one. When the rest of us are visualizing wonderful tomorrows, with the project adorned with bells, whistles and sequins, these are the ones who will keep us on track. They will keep an eye on all three sides of the project triangle, which we shall talk about in the next chapter, to make sure that no side is pulled too far out of shape in relation to the others. Your project, then, will be safe in the hands of the Here and Nows; these are the ones to whom to delegate responsibility for monitoring time and costs. They will do exactly what they agreed to do – they will be interested in the technical aspects of the project, the more detailed the better, and as long as you stick to objectives and agreed routes for getting there, these will be team players, sure of their positions in the team, sure of what to do to achieve success. Your problems with motivation will arise when changes have to be accommodated – especially sudden changes – or when they have to take on more work than they expected. It's very easy at times like this to brand them negative, or even lazy; they're not – they're extremely reliable, and your problems will be there simply because they perceive themselves to be doing a less good job than they like because of the changes.

Intuitives (Visionaries)

Those of us who are not Here and Nows take our information from visions, plans, dreams, strategies. These are great 'jam-tomorrow' people, focusing on what *will* be or *could* be. They use imagination and visioning and are very good at only 'seeing' those facts that they choose. They are often superstitious, pointing out that of course they don't really believe all that, but just in case … Needless to say, these two different personalities can drive each other mad, but every team needs at least one Visionary – unless of course it's an accounts team. Visionaries have creative ideas – often totally impossible to put into practice but not to be dismissed too lightly, since somewhere in there you'll often find the nugget of a very good idea. Visionaries are of course usually very positive – why wouldn't we be when we can always see how wonderful things are going to be when we get over this temporary hiccup?

It will be obvious that care is needed to stop the Visionary seeing her opposite number as a stick-in-the-mud, raining on everyone's parade and, in turn, being regarded as having lost touch with reality. Both have such a lot to contribute to the team – one to supply the mission and drive, the other to investigate resources that will be needed to turn the dreams into reality.

Decision-making

Decisions about these practicalities will certainly have to be made – as many as possible at the start, but some inevitably as the project progresses. Needless to say, different personalities will approach this decision-making in different ways. Jung describes these two ways of making decisions as Thinking or

Feeling and it is important to remember that this bears no reference to intelligence, education or emotion versus logic. Both personalities may be equally intelligent and make decisions equally logically.

Thinkers

Thinkers make these decisions based solely on what is good for the project's development or for the team as a whole. Their criteria tend to be efficiency, profitability, productivity and there will often be self-interest in decisions too. They are therefore valuable to the team since, having identified where they themselves want to be within the team, they will plan strategically to get there, ensuring that they are not held back on the way by the team's deviating off course. Thinkers are often ambitious, planning and sticking to their own career paths. Their downside is that they have little patience with anyone who is not so single-minded and who wants to stop to smell the roses. Although they may be regarded as uncaring, Thinkers may be very concerned indeed if people are likely to be adversely affected by a decision, but they won't let that deter them from their choice. They will become irritated and frustrated during the project if it seems you are allowing people to miss deadlines without correcting this or, say, keeping John on the project when it is obvious that he is a passenger. They may also become quite scornful of their opposites in decision-making – the Feelers.

Feelers

Feelers make decisions just as logically as Thinkers – with the difference that these decisions are almost wholly based on how they will affect people. If John is becoming a liability, the Feeler will look for ways of helping him succeed – more coaching, longer deadlines, redistribution of workload – while the Thinker is demanding his replacement. You can see the potential for misunderstanding, even conflict. The French say that 'to understand all is to forgive all'; I'm not sure I entirely agree, but do know that it is easier to be tolerant when you know why someone is acting in a particular way. The think-sheets at the end of this chapter are therefore designed to help your team members identify their own personality preferences, allowing for the fact that self-completed questionnaires are always open to our own terms of reference about ourselves and our world.

Relating to the world

Relating to the world about us, in fact, forms the basis for the fourth aspect of personality preference. How do we relate to the world – what is our preferred way of approaching it? The accepted names for the two extremes of preference are Judging and Perceptive, but these names are open to misinterpretation – 'judging', for instance, does not mean judgemental – any personality can be judgemental. Therefore I prefer to call these personality types Regulators and Flyers.

Regulators

The Regulator is the person who will be controlled all through the project by the Gantt chart and the critical path analysis that we shall look at in the next chapter. The motto 'Plan your work and work your plan' was invented for the Regulator. Once a job is started, he will want to proceed to its end without interruptions and indeed may get quite stressed if he has to interrupt one job in order to do something else. To Regulators, schedules and lists are sacrosanct and they have little patience with digressors. They will not, like the Sensates, be willing to take on the monitoring of other people – they are interested in their own progress, concerned that they themselves should reach target. You can see how they can sometimes be labelled as unco-operative when in fact they are simply focused on their own job.

The great plus about the Regulator is that you can count on him – if he says he'll be finished by Thursday, he will.

Flyers

The Flyer, on the other hand, is someone to whom spinning ten plates in the air at one time is the very stuff of life They are regarded by the Regulators as atrociously unreliable, since their (all right – our!) way of approaching a job is to pick out the bits they like and do those first, on the basis that the world may end before they reach the other bits. Thus, if asked to interrupt one task to do another, they are delighted – something else to pick the good bits from. They do ultimately finish a job – it just takes a bit longer ... The finishing is further complicated by the fact that they are reluctant to regard anything as finished in case, just as it's wrapped up, they get a better idea of how to do it. However, when they see no escape and a deadline is looming, they can work like mad and the deadline is met.

Picture, then, a project progress meeting of your team. Extrovert wants to discuss every point, Introvert says little – just scowls. Visionary is proposing some wonderful amendments to the project, Here and Now is asking tetchily where the resources are to come from. Thinker is saying that the meeting should press on without further discussion, while Feeler says that everyone is entitled to express an opinion. Regulator says she has implemented the actions agreed from last meeting and they have worked well; Flyer says he thought it was a very good idea but later had a better one, so has implemented the action but not as agreed ... Sound familiar?

Using your project to motivate differing personalities

Motivating the Extrovert

With this personality, it is important to be ready to answer questions and talk through problems (I know you don't have time, but Chapter 6 will give you some ideas on fitting this into a busy time schedule). However, since you do have time restraints, it's sometimes advisable to ask him to jot down his problem ready to talk it through – you then at least have a chance of his sticking to the point. Let him do the parts of the project which will involve discussion with other people or liaison with other departments or suppliers.

Motivating the Introvert

The Introvert will be the one to whom to give the parts of your project which can be carried out individually, not requiring too much contact with or reliance on other people. Keep an unobtrusive eye out for problems – because it may not occur to this person to discuss them with anyone else, you may not discover them until way down the line. Remember that you'll develop lasting teamwork by helping people to develop from where they are, not by trying to produce carbon copies.

Motivating the Here and Now

Try to involve your Here and Nows in as little change as possible, once you have agreed objectives and ground rules. You will be a very unusual project manager if you don't have to make changes somewhere along the line but try to leave this personality, if you can, to work through as nearly as possible to what you agreed in the beginning. Make this the person to whom progress reports are given – they will be carefully filed ready for your periodic inspection, and if you also ask this individual to let you know if anything appears to be deviating from true, you can be sure of being kept absolutely up to date.

Motivating the Visionary

You will motivate the Visionary (or 'Intuitive', to use Jung's name) by listening to her ideas, while not committing yourself to their acceptance. You will have to be careful to monitor progress, because Visionaries so often have 'Ah-hahs' in the middle of a process and decide that doing things differently will produce a much better result. They are bored by too much detail, so will often claim 'Yeah, yeah, I understand' when what they really mean is 'I can't be bothered with any more just now'. Check understanding, therefore, by questions such as: 'Just to make sure I've explained that properly, tell me how you've understood it', or 'What impression have I given you about … ?'. This technique of suggesting that in fact it might be your communication skills that are at fault stops the defensive 'Do you think I'm a fool?' response, when you may well have to bite your lip!

Motivating the Thinker

This is the person to involve in strategic planning of your project, risk assessment or budgetary forecasts since, as we have seen, she will not be swayed by anything which may hamper progress. Beware, though, that she does not demotivate other people by expecting unrealistic standards.

Motivating the Feeler

Because the Feeler cares so much about people, you will have to take great care to explain to him exactly why you are having to take some decisions which may affect other people adversely. However, strike a happy medium between explanations and justifications – you do not have time constantly to be justifying yourself, nor is it appropriate from a management point of view that you should always be doing so. There will be times when 'This is what we have to do if we want to bring this project home on time' will have to be enough.

Motivating the Regulator

Since it is rare, in today's working environment, that you can always allow time to finish one task before starting on another, the Regulator may sometimes be difficult to keep fully motivated. If she is an Extrovert, she will complain loud and long when she has to interrupt a task; the Introvert will just go tight-lipped and slam things about! Make sure you take a minute to explain why you are asking for the task to be interrupted, and wherever possible try not to take the 'and-another-thing' approach, loading the Regulator down with what she will perceive to be an impossibly long list of things to be done.

Motivating the Flyer

Just give the Flyer as many different jobs as you can – but be careful. You are delighted to have someone to whom to delegate; she is delighted to have another task to do – just be aware of the 'willing horse' syndrome. There will come a time when she absolutely must finish some of the tasks she already has before you allow her to accept any more.

The reality is, of course, that if you are to achieve your objective of developing teamwork, everyone has to accept that a particular personality cannot be allowed free rein all the time. Understanding your personality type explains why you prefer to work in one way; it doesn't excuse behaviour which refuses to see things from any point of view but its own. We can all act 'out of personality' when appropriate – for instance, if I've promised a client a training proposal by Wednesday he expects to receive it, not a message to say I'm delaying sending it in case I get a better idea. There are times when you, a Regulator, have to stop what you are doing and go and help one of your team; and when it comes to solving problems, you need to let two extremes of your personality come into play, so that you look at the problem and assimilate all the facts as a Here and Now, then bring the creative Visionary part of you into play, take a look as a Feeler at how this will affect people, and come to a final decision as a Thinker. If you have to act out of personality too often, though, it will feel as if you're wearing someone else's shoes and it will be uncomfortable. I believe a lot of stress in today's workplace comes from having to wear a behaviour style which is foreign to you. If you're wanting your people to knit a team, encourage toleration for 'different strokes for different folks'.

The motivational ladder

As team leader, you will not only have to motivate each personality, you will have to motivate each person on his/her rung of the 'motivational ladder'. You will almost certainly know about Maslow's Hierarchy of Motivational Needs, which he portrayed as a triangle, with basic motivational needs forming a broad base and 'self-fulfilment' at the pinnacle. His theory is that, until an individual's motivational needs are met at one level, he or she will not be motivated at a higher level; this was recognized long before Maslow by William Booth, the Victorian social reformer and founder of the Salvation Army, who opened soup-kitchens because he said that, 'It's no good talking to a man about his soul if his belly is empty'. I prefer to portray this succession of motivational needs as a staircase rather than a triangle since I think it reminds us that, like your investments, motivation can go down as well as up. Maslow represented the base of his triangle as the basic needs to sustain life – air, water, food, room to live. (He also included sex, but I'm reluctant to mention that in case this is not a good time for you and you blame that for your demotivation.) Everyone who works for you will have these basic needs fulfilled, although you will have seen how, when redundancies are in the air, people who are motivated at a very high level will go right back down to 'Will I

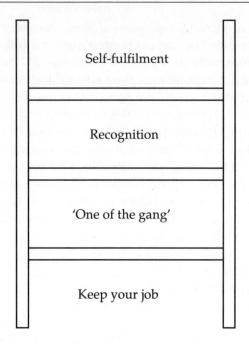

Figure 2.1   The motivational ladder

be able to live if I lose my job? Will I be able to feed the family? Will I lose my house?' My workplace motivational ladder (Figure 2.1) starts at the next level up – Maslow's 'Safety and Security' level.

Exploring the ladder

Hopefully, very few of your team will be operating at the 'keep your job' level. However, it is very easy, if you yourself are excited about the project and are caught up in it, to forget that some people come to work solely to earn money to support their life outside work. Those of us who are fortunate enough to enjoy what we do, and to whom work is in fact an important part of our life, need to remember that not everyone sees it that way. If someone is motivated on the first rung of this ladder, accept it and make sure that they are working to an acceptable standard which, insofar as is within your power, will secure their job.

They may in fact be between rungs one and two – a foot on each, as it were. The second rung is, to my mind, the dangerous one. If someone is motivated by belonging – being one of the gang – motivation will wear very thin if lack of communication means that this person perceives a degree of exclusion: 'they never tell us anything', 'we're just cogs in a very large wheel'. I was working at one time with the managers of a very large organization which had formerly been nationalized. At the beginning of the third day's training, one of the managers burst in shouting; 'Have you seen this?' There, as tabloid headlines, was news of very significant changes due to happen in the organization – and this was the first that any of these managers had heard of it! Immediately, all conversation became: 'Some of us will be going', 'They won't need all of us', as the motivation almost visibly sank down a rung.

There is another reason for my thinking that this is the dangerous rung. If it's very important to you that you're one of the gang – indeed, this is the main reason you stay here, when you could earn more elsewhere – and all the corporate self-talk in that department is negative, bad-mouthing the organization, the managers, the customers, then you'll join in and help spread that negativity. It will come naturally to do this if you're going to stay one of the gang. If, however, the corporate self-talk is positive, directed towards solving problems and making things better, then you'll join in with that positivism. I therefore have a question – what is the corporate self-talk like in your team?

The big danger in leading people who are operating on the top rungs of the ladder is that because they are working well you are tempted to think you can leave them to it with no need for praise. This is very understandable – it's such a relief not to have to watch over someone all the time, especially if some other team members are time-consuming. However, people motivated on the third rung need recognition in order to stay there, if they are not to fall back a rung and join in the 'you could die here and nobody would care, never a thank you' talk. So – another question – how free are you with your thankyous or well-dones, and how much is it going to cost you to give them this recognition? (All right, that's two questions – I'm a trainer, not a mathematician.) I'm not suggesting you flood them with saccharine – no one needs that unless he or she is feeling very insecure – but just the occasional acknowledgement of effort or achievement will stop the slide. Instead, they'll progress to the top of the ladder, where they do a good job for its own sake, they work extra time because 'that's what they do'. Why on earth does anyone want to run a marathon, or collect for charity, or spend a weekend clearing up the environment? Simply because 'it's what they do'. It would be wonderful if all your team were working at this level and they'll only progress there if you give them motivation all the way up the ladder.

Motivating each rung

- On the bottom rung, accept them for what they are, value them for the fact that they will work hard enough and effectively enough to keep their job but don't spend a lot of your management time trying to make them into something they are not. If they are performing well at this level, leave them to it; if not, see some ideas in Chapter 6 for dealing with poor performers.
- On the second rung, make sure that communication is as faultless as you can manage; avoid favouritism; encourage positive corporate self-talk.
- On the third rung, be sure that good work is recognized, preferably publicly; remember to thank them for any extra effort; give them a little extra authority if that is at all possible, maybe making them responsible for the implementation of part of the project.
- On the top rung, avoid constant looking over their shoulder – they will do the job and do it well, because it's what they do. Just remember that even at this level recognition is welcome from time to time.

Motivating yourself

Just one more thing before we leave this; I'm often asked 'Who motivates the motivator?' The answer, I'm afraid, is the motivator! As team leader, you're responsible for keeping yourself motivated – you owe it to yourself and your team.

We've looked at the importance of encouraging positive corporate self-talk; it's just as important that you control your personal self-talk. Give yourself credit for what's going right, look at hiccups in a 'how can I solve this?' way rather than a 'Here we go again' fashion. When you make a horrendous mistake, tell yourself quickly 'That's not like me' rather than 'Trust me to screw things up!'. Recognize your own motivational rung on the ladder and decide whether you want to move up one. Apply the same criteria to your own motivation as you do to other people's. Identify just why you really stay in the job, when it may well be that you could move if you wanted to, and, insofar as you can, make sure you repeat for yourself motivating experiences. Your own motivation is vital to the success of your team – you're the one who will have to lead all the planning and implementation that we shall discuss in the next chapter.

Personality profile

Explain to each team member that this is an exercise designed to facilitate working together on the project by identifying how each person prefers to approach different aspects of the task.

For each statement, put a tick under the number on the scale closest to your perception of yourself, with 1 being most like you, and 5 being least like you; for instance, in the first question in section I, if you usually like variety and action but sometimes like to be quiet and concentrate, you would put your tick under the first 3 or 4; if it's the other way around, you'd put your tick under the second 3 or 4; if, however, you always like variety and action, your tick would be under the first 1. Too many 5s says you're kidding yourself – no one can be that well balanced! Count up your scores (which will be the number of ticks under A, the left-hand side, and B, the right-hand side) at the end of each section separately, and compare with the interpretation at the end of the section.

A   B

1 2 3 4 5 4 3 2 1

I   Recharging your batteries

I like variety and action	I like to concentrate quietly
I quite like telephone interruptions	I dislike any interruptions
I like to work with people	I like to get on with work alone
I communicate well	I have problems in communicating
I like to discuss problems	I keep my problems to myself
I am curious about other people	I just get on with my own life
I prefer verbal communication	I prefer memos or e-mail
I often speak without thinking	I choose my words carefully
I like to learn by experience	I like to understand an experience

II   Absorbing information

I am realistic about work forecasting	I am hazy about time-scales
I like to work routinely	I like to work innovatively
I like to use existing skills	I like to learn new skills to use
I am good at detailed work	I grow impatient with detail
I work steadily through a task	I tend to work in bursts
I seldom trust my inspiration	I follow my inspiration
I usually get facts right	I often muddle facts
I like to focus on my part of a task	I like to see the overall picture

III   Making decisions

Truth is important to me	I like to embroider the truth
I am unaffected by office feuds	I like harmony around me
I take impersonal decisions	I consider people's wishes

Reproduced from *Developing Teams Through Project-Based Learning*, Jean Atkinson, Gower, Aldershot, 2001.

A   B
1 2 3 4 5 4 3 2 1

I have no problem in reprimanding	I dislike reprimanding
I need fair treatment	I need praise
I relate best to people like me	I relate well to most people
I am told I am often tactless	I take care what I say
I can identify problems early	I often overlook problems

IV   Relating to the world

I like to plan and stick to my plan	I keep all options open
I make quick decisions	I decide carefully
I like to start and finish a project	I work on several projects
I work sequentially through	I pick out parts to work on
I am glad when I finish	I like ongoing projects
I like to choose my experiences	I welcome most experiences
I like to control life	I like to enjoy life

Interpretation

Check in which column, A or B, the majority of your ticks appeared.

Recharging your batteries:	Column A, Extrovert	Column B, Introvert
Absorbing information:	Column A, Here and Now	Column B, Visionary
Making decisions:	Column A, Thinker	Column B, Feeler
Relating to the world:	Column A, Regulator	Column B, Flyer

Self-motivation profile

This exercise is to help you identify where each of your team is on the motivation ladder, so that as far as possible you can meet them where they are. When each member has completed it, take time to discuss it one-to-one.

Score a tick under the number which you think most describes you – 1 low, 10 high.

1 2 3 4 5 6 7 8 9 10

Money is the most important thing to me
Regular hours are essential
My physical working environment is important

I like to socialize with workmates outside work
I believe regular team meetings are important
I think a company newsletter is important

Promotion prospects are important to me
I believe all managers should have an office
I prefer not to call the MD by a first name

Variety is more important than money
I like work which stretches me
I like to work outside my job description

Interpretation
Check where your highest scores are:
First trio – 'Keep your job' level
Second trio – 'One of the gang' level
Third trio – Recognition and status level
Fourth trio – Self-fulfilment level

Reproduced from *Developing Teams Through Project-Based Learning*,
Jean Atkinson, Gower, Aldershot, 2001.

3 Developing planning skills

The objectives of this chapter are:

1 To help you recognize a poorly planned project.
2 To help you set objectives for your own project.
3 To introduce the project triangle.
4 To remind you of the five factors which will motivate your team to come along with you on the project.
5 To show an effective way of preparing a list of tasks and activities.
6 To remind you of a possible need for training as part of your planning.

Important question – what is this project *for*?

A poorly planned project

At one time in my life I taught junior school (I only stuck it for four years, and it has left me with an enormous respect for teachers who do it all their lives). It was before the days of the national curriculum and, one spring morning, the teacher who was in charge of maths throughout the school announced in the staffroom that he had planned a project for the children for that day and he asked for our co-operation. For an hour, all the children would combine forces to work out the area of the school playground and playing field. First-years would measure the length of their feet and then use that measurement to pace out the width and breadth of the lawn; second-years would measure the playground area with click-wheels; third-years would use tape-measures to calculate the areas of the drive and carpark; fourth-years would assess the area of the playing field using tape-measures. To say we were gobsmacked would be an understatement. There were three classes in each year, each of around thirty children. Imagine the chaos. One teacher immediately withdrew co-operation, but capitulated to blackmail about her class being the only ones not enjoying the sunshine. 'But what is the objective of it all?', we wanted to know. 'To teach them to calculate area of course', came the reply.

I'm ashamed to say we all gave in. I don't need to describe the confusion. After about fifteen minutes, some us decided we'd had enough; after about half an hour, everyone was back in their classrooms. At breaktime we all took our classes' woefully inadequate and meaningless figures to the staffroom to ask our colleague what he wanted to do with them next. 'Oh', he said airily, 'I'm not going to do your maths lessons for you – use them as you think fit'. There were a lot of full waste-paper baskets that day.

Why did this project fail? For one thing, no thought had been given to planning – the idea seemed to have been 'It's a nice day – let's take the children outside'. For another, there was no attempt to get people's commitment. There was a lack of accountability on the part of the project's sponsor, the maths specialist; and no one could answer the question 'What is it *for*?' Unfortunately, this situation is mirrored in so many projects in the business world where no one has thought to ask that question.

Smart objectives

Given the title of this book, you might assume that the answer to the question has to be 'to develop teamwork'. However, while this is your primary objective, there have to be other measurable objectives which will indicate success. At the end of it, the participants need to be able to say not just 'We are working as a team' but 'This is what we have achieved by working as a team'. You may well be familiar with the idea that any objective must be SMART:

Specific
Measurable
Achievable
Realistic
Time-related

Specific
What exactly will success look like? For instance, we want not only to complete the project successfully, but also on time, within the time-scale and to the standard agreed. Be sure, then, that not only are you clear about what success will look like but you have communicated this properly to the rest of the team as well.

Measurable
This really follows on from the last paragraph – the team must be able to measure success. This is why it's no good simply setting 'improve teamwork' as your goal. Start off with a brainstorming session beginning; 'We shall know we're really working as a team when ...'

However, with this particular objective in mind you may simply want to discuss measurable project objectives without mentioning your own agenda to improve teamwork in case the perception is: 'We're all right as we are'. When, at the end of the project, better teamwork has in fact been achieved then the post-mortem might be the time to add: 'One of the things I was hoping this project would do was to get us working more as a team; I think we've achieved this, because ... ', and give some examples.

Achievable

Contrary to what, I'm sad to say, some managers would still have you believe, there is no motivation in setting targets or objectives which are just out of reach. I know – I've also heard 'Aim at the moon and you might hit the housetops' and I think it's tripe! It sets you up for failure and dangerously gives you a cop-out when you fail. Why not aim for the housetops in the first place and then use that success as a launch-pad to the moon? If you ask people to be involved in a project for which the time-scale and budget are so unreasonable as to make it unachievable to the required standard, you'll certainly get united participants – they'll be united in demotivation, demoralization, whingeing and copping out. This is not the kind of teamwork you had in mind.

Realistic

This is not quite the same as achievable – indeed, it can almost be the reverse. What may be a realistic expectation of Paul, who has only been in the department a few weeks and who doesn't have wide experience of the work, might be unrealistic for Pauline, who has been with the organization for five years, in this department for two and who can realistically be expected to produce a different level of work in terms of both time and quality. If you feel, when you are agreeing objectives, that Pauline is setting her sights too low, then make her justify her level of expectation of herself; and if Paul, in an attempt to stay 'one of the gang', sets himself objectives you perceive to be unrealistic, then also make him justify – don't encourage him to set himself up for failure. If you make people justify their commitment to what they think they can achieve, you are of course removing their cop-outs. If they don't manage what they said they could, and you discuss your disappointment with them, they can never use the excuse, 'Well, it was an unrealistic target anyway'.

Time-related

'A dream with a time limit is an objective.' Everybody needs dreams, every project manager needs objectives – don't confuse the two! As part of your measurement process, you must be able to plan and monitor time, and we shall look at ways of dealing with this in the next chapter.

The project triangle

'Time', in fact, forms one of the sides of the all-important project triangle, around which any project is built (Figure 3.1).

Figure 3.1   The project triangle

Suppose your department has agreed to carry out a project to discover why the company has lost some of its important customers. You have agreed with the marketing director – the project's sponsor – that you will put two people on the project, for six months, to contact all current and former customers to find out how, in their view, your service could improve. You have also agreed to a weekly progress meeting with the sponsor. The cost will be the salaries of these two people plus phone calls; you have agreed on £20,000, which will be booked to the marketing budget. Your project triangle will look as shown in Figure 3.2.

However, you and the sponsor decide after a month that six months is, after all, too long – you need to get this through before staff holidays start in earnest. You will therefore put more people on the project and get it finished within four months. The cost side stays the same, since you will be using the same number of staff hours as originally budgeted – you will just

Quality
All customers contacted,
weekly progress meetings

Figure 3.2   The project triangle – example 1

telescope them. The time side obviously alters. Both you and
your sponsor are finding weekly meetings more difficult than
you expected, so you agree that you will submit written progress
reports weekly. Your project triangle is now as shown in Figure
3.3.

The concept of the project triangle becomes enormously
important when the sponsor wants to change agreed specifications. He can have almost any changes he wants, but it may
take longer and cost more; or if she wants to renegotiate costs,
this is not a problem provided that she accepts that it may take a
little longer and quality specifications may have to be a little
lower. You need to be realistic about all three sides right at the
beginning. Within this triangle, anything at all is possible – if
your budget is unlimited and you have years to bring the project
home, you can agree to wonderful objectives around standards
of quality. If, like most of us, you're on a limited, strictly agreed
budget, and you're having to carry on with your everyday work
whilst the project is in progress, then look carefully at what you
are agreeing to regarding standards of success. You may be
interested to know that a study at the University of Arizona
identified the fact that undue optimism at the planning stage of
a project was far more likely to result in an unsatisfactory

Figure 3.3   The project triangle – example 2

outcome than any technical problems that the project might encounter. I also believe strongly that it's better to delay the start of a project for a few days with concomitant adjustments to finishing time, so that you start well prepared with all participants knowing their roles, rather than be pressurized into starting before you're clear in your own mind how you want this to progress. You may well have to 'sell' the idea of the project to the people you want to knit into the team. It's essential that you be able to present the benefit and rationale of the project, and you can't do this if you're not quite clear in your own mind.

Getting the team on your side

When you first present the project to your team, it's worth remembering that most people will make a decision based on emotional reasons, and justify it to themselves on logical reasons. The five main decision-making motives are: financial gain, safety, ego, comfort, appeal. Appeal is by far the most common motive – just think this one through. You know that if you are due to go on holiday next week and your car's tyres are dangerously worn, you will tell yourself that you will get the tyres fixed when you can afford them; you won't, unless you are very unusual, spend your holiday money on a new set of tyres! The 'appeal' of the holiday will win out over the 'safety' aspect of getting your tyres fixed. You will probably justify it to yourself along the lines of 'I really need this holiday – I've been working hard and I really need this break to maintain my efficiency', the implication being that you will suffer burnout if you keep going ... then you'll lose your job ... You've justified your emotional decision on logical grounds. Surprisingly, it has been found that the order of motivation for a decision is: appeal, comfort, ego, safety, financial considerations – yes, I know, I was surprised at the last one too! (If you question the 'ego, safety' order, just ask yourself: if expense were no object, would you go for a flashy car or a safe one?)

Anyway, this means that when you introduce the project to your people, you need to find aspects that will sound good to the participants and will not appear to be too much hassle if you want them to come along with you. Will there be kudos for the team in completing the project? Will it provide a comfortable work environment, lessening the current sniping that is spoiling good teamwork? Will improved efficiency mean that jobs are more secure? Will there be a bonus at the end of it? Remember that your motivation may be different from theirs; you may want the satisfaction of researching something; they may see it as just another chore in addition to their regular work. Therefore, if you want to take them with you, it's worth taking time to identify ways of making the project more appealing.

Task analysis

So, you've set your objectives; you've identified the three sides of your triangle; you've identified which of those sides can be slightly flexible if necessary; you've identified benefits to present to your people. You're ready to look at what needs to be done in the project, and who is the best person to do it.

Even in these hi-tech days, I don't think you can beat the 'sticky-note' method – using those sticky-topped squares that we all use to leave messages for ourselves everywhere. This is definitely a team task: however thorough you are yourself, it's fatally easy to miss out a vital step which will throw your whole timing into chaos later on. The sticky-note approach is really a variation on brainstorming, with the difference being that the notes can be moved around as necessary. The procedure is as simple as brainstorming:

1   Give each team member a small pad of sticky notes.
2   Ask each person to think of tasks which will need to be done in the course of the project and to write one idea on each piece of paper – no particular order, just as they come to mind.
3   As each task is written, stick the note on a flip-chart or wall.
4   Repeat until everyone has come up with all the ideas he/she can think of.
5   Group into lists of tasks and activities. A task is a major event, an activity is a contributory event; for instance, if you want to post a letter, the tasks would be folding the letter, putting it into an envelope, attaching the stamp, putting it into the box; activities would be picking up the letter to fold, finding the envelope and addressing it, finding the stamp, licking the stamp, walking to the post-box.

Here's how your list might proceed. You've decided you want to develop your customer-care team via a project. Your objective is:

Three months from now we want to be co-operating well, willing to help each other with workloads, ready to share ideas and information. We want an atmosphere in which no one blames anyone else but where all take accountability for their own mistakes. We want to be more concerned with putting things right than with pointing the finger. As a result of, and contributing to, this we want a department where phones are answered within three rings, all customers' queries and complaints are passed to the relevant department within an hour, and the person who took the initial call gets back to the customer within three days to check progress and satisfaction.

First of all, you'll discuss objectives with your staff – as has already been mentioned, you might at this stage want to concentrate on the practical aspects of the project: improved customer care. When they have all sticky-noted, the wall or flip-chart might look as shown in Figure 3.4.

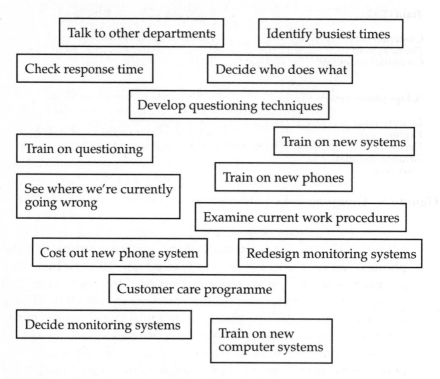

Figure 3.4   The sticky-note approach

Grouping tasks and activities

The next step is to group under tasks and activities, as in Figure 3.5.

You will see that there is as yet no time-scale attached to any of this – we're still at the early planning stage and specific times come a little later. Talking of time, when are you going to get time to do all this with your team? Well, how about devoting your next team meeting to it? It will be more motivational than

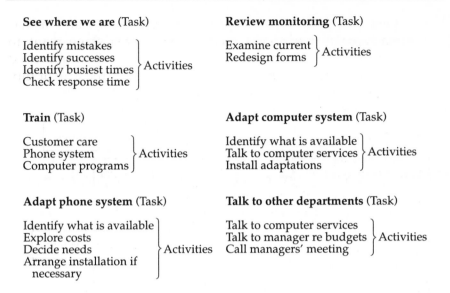

See where we are (Task)

Identify mistakes ⎫
Identify successes ⎬ Activities
Identify busiest times ⎰
Check response time ⎭

Review monitoring (Task)

Examine current ⎱ Activities
Redesign forms ⎰

Train (Task)

Customer care ⎫
Phone system ⎬ Activities
Computer programs ⎭

Adapt computer system (Task)

Identify what is available ⎫
Talk to computer services ⎬ Activities
Install adaptations ⎭

Adapt phone system (Task)

Identify what is available ⎫
Explore costs ⎪
Decide needs ⎬ Activities
Arrange installation if ⎪
  necessary ⎭

Talk to other departments (Task)

Talk to computer services ⎫
Talk to manager re budgets ⎬ Activities
Call managers' meeting ⎭

Figure 3.5   Grouping tasks and activities

telling them yet again they're taking too long to answer the phones! Another alternative is to take people off the phone two or three at a time, with the rest covering for them. The last group gets to arrange the stickies the others have left. This is obviously less satisfactory than having everyone buzzing at the same time but we need to accept we're living in the real world. I am aware that in a busy department this places extra strain on people who are having to cover for each other, but it is only for a short time and it's an investment of time in order to use it more effectively in the future.

Let's look at these tasks and activities; some of them will almost certainly be shared with your own project, however large or small.

See where we are

It's at the 'See where we are' stage that you may find defensiveness. If the culture of the organization up to now has been one of blame, people may perceive that this is yet another way of seeing what they're doing wrong. It's sad when a cycle is established in an organization of blame, defensiveness, low motivation, poor performance, blame. Your objective for your team in this project, whether or not you have expressed this to them at the beginning, is to establish a benign circle of 'How can we put it right?' 'What have we learnt from it?' 'Accountability, motivation, improvement'. Therefore it's very important to stress that what you're after is the facts as they are – their acceptability or otherwise is not the question and no one need make excuses for, for example, the current call-rate. I am reminded of a branch manager of mine when I was regional director of a sales organization. When, at monthly meetings, I asked for sales forecasts for the next month, his were always glowing: he had firm expectations from company A, company B, company XYZ. It took me a few months to realize that this was defensive, wishful thinking on his part, and even longer to convince him that I couldn't help him over a slow sales month if I didn't know one was coming up. My accountability became closer monitoring and more help with his planning. You can't expect your project to stay on course if you're receiving inaccurate data, either at the beginning or as things progress.

Liaison

Successful liaison with other departments will also be important to your success. Try, at meetings with other department heads who may be affected by your project, to use a forward-looking, problem-solving approach: 'We want to do this because ... but we do realize that this may cost you some time and trouble. What hiccups can you envisage and how can we help you get round them?' If, at every problem raised – and again, we live in the real world where most organizations have at least one Jobsworth who almost as a reflex seems to greet any new idea negatively – you can take this 'How can we help?' approach, rather than getting into a 'you-can-you-can't' situation, you're much more likely to overcome his/her cop-outs. It may even be that something in the system that you had not foreseen will come up, and you will have to re-jig your own thinking accordingly.

Training as part of preparation

The project we're using as an example may involve some training on customer care, questioning techniques, handling priorities, just as in your own workplace your project may involve training.

This can be achieved by other group training or on a one-to-one basis, and can be delivered in-house or on 'open courses'. It's worth giving a little consideration to the best way of doing things for your own team members – just because the organization has always used The Training Company doesn't mean that you need to go to the expense of The Training Company this time; would it be better to provide this particular training in-house? Let's look briefly at some points you need to be aware of, starting with external courses.

Open programmes

Some companies have salespeople who sell the courses but do not deliver the training; these people should be able to answer all your questions to your satisfaction. If they can't, try another company – goodness knows there are enough of us! In other cases, trainers themselves both sell and present the courses. Beware wild claims about what 'your people will be able to do' by the end of the course; all any external 'open' programme can guarantee is that information will be presented in a way which makes learning and retention easy, by trainers with a wide experience of both training and their subject. I would always want to know where the trainer had got the knowledge – whether in the real world or all from books. The use to which delegates put the knowledge they gain is to a very large extent dependent on how you, the manager, prepare, debrief and follow up.

Before the delegate goes on the course, discuss the syllabus in the light of his or her training needs and the needs of the project, advising on the points which will be specially relevant. There may well be parts which do not apply directly to your business – this is inevitable since an open programme needs to cover as broad a canvas as possible. This will be compensated for by the fact that your delegate will meet and exchange ideas with others from a wide variety of backgrounds, who will be experiencing the same problems and successes as your team member. Urge your person to consider carefully all ideas before deciding that 'that won't work in our company'. It's much more cost-effective to ask 'How would we need to adapt that before it would work for us?'

Delegates are often met on their return with: 'Good course, was it? Learn a lot?' This does nothing to reinforce the learning and, as training is never cheap, it's worth taking a little trouble to debrief properly. Go through the syllabus with them session by session: 'What was the content? How does it apply to your project? What will you change from your current way of working? What help will you need to put it into practice?'

Internal training

Of course, it may well not be necessary to use external trainers at all – it may be that an hour with someone from another department who is already using your planned system will be effective. Or perhaps someone from the department which will be affected by your project needs to come and explain the effect that a change in the established system will have on that department, the problems that might occur and how they can best be tackled. A spin-off from your own objective of improving teamwork among your own people might be an improvement in inter-departmental teamwork, through a better understanding of how other departments work and the difficulties that each – albeit unwittingly – can cause the other. Don't take it for granted that your own team realizes the effect that the success of your project may well have on, for instance, the accounts department or the dispatch department.

Remember the sides of the triangle – time, cost, quality. You will need to be able constantly and clearly to ensure that budgets are not being exceeded, that you are where you planned to be and the project so far is producing acceptable results. Without regular monitoring it is very easy for a project to slip and – possibly even more dangerous for teamwork – staff to become demotivated because what was billed as being so important at the beginning is now perceived to be of little value after all. Those lists of tasks and activities that we looked at need some time references attached. It's time we studied some ways of monitoring.

What is this project for?

For discussion with your team

Our specific objectives are:

We shall complete these by:

Therefore we need to start by:

What will success look like?

Our project triangle will be:

You will almost certainly take the decisions on this yourself, but check with the team that these decisions are realistic.

Time:

Cost:

Quality of outcome:

The three sides can be flexible to this extent:

Time:

Cost:

Quality of outcome:

Other people our project may affect are

Use this with your team to stress right from the beginning the fact that your project will almost certainly not be carried out in isolation.

Person   Department   Effect   We can help by

Reproduced from *Developing Teams Through Project-Based Learning,*
Jean Atkinson, Gower, Aldershot, 2001.

4 Developing monitoring skills

This chapter's objectives are:

1 To help you to estimate time and budgets needed for your project.
2 To introduce project management charts.
3 To remind you of the importance of monitoring individual performance.
4 To suggest ways of bringing poor performers up to standard to progress your project.

If each side of your project triangle is flexible, allowing time, cost and quality to be amended as necessary, then it's essential to keep a watchful eye on each side to identify early on which one needs tweaking. It would be wonderful if all our projects sailed through without a hitch, but we live in the real world where Murphy's Law rules, and we know that a dropped slice of bread will always land butter-side down! We need to be able to deflect the slice in mid-air, so that even if it's still going to fall, at least it will be butter-side up. Therefore some assessment of risk will always need to be built into our planning, with every team member accepting responsibility for reporting to the project manager immediately if time or budget look like slipping.

Time estimations

Don't ever allow yourself to be cajoled into unrealistic estimation of the time needed for any part of the project. Staff in one of my client companies complained recently that when their manager asks: 'How long will this task take?' and they say 'Five days', the answer is always 'Well, I want it in three'. They shrug, the task takes five days, the manager says that it's not good enough – and for the next task the whole project repeats itself. Every member of staff is thereby being set up for constant failure. Since you'll never get the best out of a team which regards itself as a failure, it's imperative that time be calculated realistically. The other very important point to take on board is that your quoted budget will depend on staff hours committed, so that the cost and time sides of your triangle are very closely related.

When calculating time needed, you will of course talk to other people who have undertaken a similar project, add on 25 per cent for bragging, and add on another 25 per cent for the 'just in case' factor. However, there is an accepted formula for calculating time needed for anything:

$$\frac{Top + (4Tml) + Twc}{6}$$

where:

Top is optimistic time – if there were no glitches at all, this is the least time it could take.

Twc is worst case time – if everything goes wrong.

Tml is most likely time, realistically.

I'm sure the mathematicians among you will be able to tell me why you divide by six, and indeed why this formula works at all; the rest of us just regard formulae as a gift from heaven and give thanks for them! It was taught to me years ago and I have to say I've found it works beautifully.

Risk assessment

Don't forget the 'what-if' factor when calculating *Twc*. You can't possibly allow for everything that might happen, otherwise you'd never start a project at all. The negative people on your team will always be able to think of something awful that might happen – I call this the wild Mongolian ostrich syndrome – suppose a herd of wild Mongolian ostriches rushes into the office in the middle of the project! However, sensible risk assessment is vital; if there's a real chance of something happening to delay your project – a strike which will affect deliveries to your suppliers, for instance – then that needs to be built into your worst-case time. The risks for which to plan strategically are those that are quite likely to occur and that will have a strong impact on your project if they happen – for example, one of your team who is pregnant will not be leaving till the project is finished but may well have to take time off for clinics. Then there are the risks which are unlikely to happen but would impact on your project if they did – a key member leaving during the project, perhaps – and some which are very likely to happen but which will have little effect on your project, such as a team member going on holiday, when his work can be covered quite easily. The strategies for coping, then, need to be planned around the first two: high impact, high risk and high impact, low risk. You need to consider how each of these will affect time-scales and budgets.

Budget planning

Budgets are going to be a key factor, of course, whether the project is client-generated or whether you are simply carrying it out within the team. Include all costs in your estimate: staff hours, delivery costs, overtime, raw materials, use of machinery, and, if the project is likely to generate a lot of paperwork, the cost of the paper. I know this last seems negligible, but as someone whose training programmes take a lot of paper for hand-outs, I know what an expense this can be. Make sure you get input at this stage from each team member as to time estimates, and ask for justification of any which seem unduly high or low.

Project management charts

Having examined overall time-scale and costs, you'll need to decide how you will monitor progress and how much of this you will need to do yourself; this may be an excellent opportunity to develop teamwork by delegating responsibility for ongoing monitoring to a member of staff, while you yourself review everything on a regular but less frequent basis. Ensure that the delegatee knows the importance of immediately bringing to your attention any falling behind.

Two charts which are accepted as standard in planning and monitoring are the Gantt chart and the critical path analysis (CPA); some people use both, some find one or the other works best for them. I must admit that, because I hate charts that look like charts, I tend towards the critical path analysis, but you may feel quite differently.

Gantt charts

You will remember that in Chapter 3 we had the wall littered with sticky-notes, which we put into lists, not necessarily in order of doing, and to which we added no time-scales. Gantt charts and CPA take these tasks, lay them out in sequence and attach time-scales. (In case you are wondering why it's called a Gantt Chart, it was first devised in 1917 by a man called Henry Gantt.)

Figure 4.1 is a sample Gantt chart for the project we were looking at in the last chapter. The lists we had there, repeated so that you don't have to keep turning back, and put into a rough running order were:

See where we are	Talk to other department
Identify mistakes and successes	Talk to computer services
Identify busiest times	Talk re budgets
Check current response times	Call a management meeting

Activity	Start date	End date	Duration	Time scale				
				w/c:1/4	8/4	15/4	22/4	29/4
Identify current probs.	1/4	5/4	5 days					
Examine and re-design forms	8/4	9/4	2 days					
Explore phones	8/4	12/4	5 days					
Talk to computer s'vces	8/4	8/4	1 day					
Decide phones	9/4	9/4	1 day					
Discuss budgets	9/4	9/4	1 day					
Call meeting	10/4	10/4	1 day					
Install program	15/4	15/4	1 day					
Install phones	22/4	22/4	1 day					
Train staff	23/4	25/4	3 days					

Figure 4.1   Sample Gantt chart

Review monitoring
Examine current
Re-design as necessary

Adapt computer program
Identify needs
Talk to services
Install adaptations

Adapt phone system
Identify what's available
Explore costs
Decide needs
Arrange installation if appropriate

Train staff
Customer care
Questioning skills
Phone systems
Computer systems

I call this a rough running order because it is obvious that some activities from each task can be carried out simultaneously by different people, while with others there is a definite hierarchy – this one cannot take place until that has been completed. Now you have your rough running order, you can construct your Gantt chart. To do this:

● List all tasks and activities.
● Decide on a 'running order' – which tasks must precede and follow others?
● Estimate time required for each activity, and therefore for each task.
● Decide on a start date, in order to fulfil your agreed finishing date.
● Draw up your chart.

Critical path analysis
While some people swear by the Gantt chart to plot their projects, others, as I have mentioned, find that they have drawbacks. Some of us just do not like charts; some like to use a tool which makes it clear immediately which resources, human or otherwise, are available to progress a project on a certain date. These latter feel that a critical path analysis suits their way of working better and, as has already been mentioned, some people like to use both, using the Gantt chart as a set-up tool and then using the critical path analysis (usually known as the CPA) as an everyday working tool. One of the great advantages of the CPA is that it helps you monitor the actual number of staff days needed for a project and thus helps with

the budget-setting. It shows you easily which tasks can be done while others are taking place and which have to wait for others' completion, providing almost a pictorial record of the project's planning. If you add the names of the people who will actually be doing the tasks, you can quickly ensure that no one is overloaded and that everyone is being given an opportunity to contribute. It helps, too, with risk management – John may have to have treatment for his back during the project, so let's not give him a task which is crucial to progress and let's make sure that someone else will be free to take on his part if necessary. Compile your CPA by:

- listing all activities and tasks
- identifying those which can be done simultaneously
- deciding which must be completed before others can take place
- assigning a name to each task
- drawing up your CPA plan.

The CPA for the project we're imagining could look like Figure 4.2.

The budgetary control form
With a Gantt chart, CPA form and a budgetary control form, you can keep a careful eye on your project's progress. A budgetary control form is the simplest of the lot – just a very simple graph plotting actual expenditure against your estimations (Figure 4.3).

As you see, the expenditure in this chart is just at the stage where the project manager will need to keep an eye on things. He or she would be wise at this point to sit down with all expenditure records and check back through to see where the money has gone. It may well be that there is nothing to worry about – maybe there was an unexpected rise in staff costs at the end of month 3, with contract staff having to augment the regular team for a short while, because set-up had taken longer than planned. The manager will have to be aware, though, that there is less slack in the system now for anything else to go wrong and be coped with, and unless a way can be found for recouping the money overspent, it may be advisable to speak to the sponsor

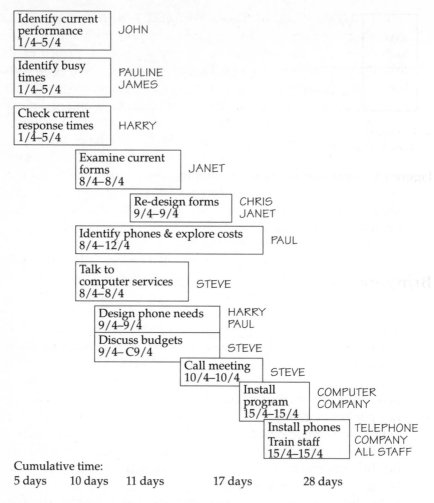

Figure 4.2   **Sample critical path analysis**

straightaway. Of course you can monitor expenditure without a chart – you can simply check on all written records on a regular basis – but this is such a useful pictorial tool which can be used not only by the manager but by the rest of the team as well. It is just the simplest way to see how you're doing and to take remedial steps. If you've wildly underestimated it means you can re-negotiate immediately with the client and, equally important, it means that your team also accepts accountability for budgetary control, since they can see straightaway where

	Month 1	Month 2	Month 3	Month 4	Month 5	Month 6
4000						
3000						
2000						
1000						

Estimated expenditure ---------------
Actual expenditure ⎯⎯⎯⎯⎯⎯

Figure 4.3   Sample budgetary control form

slippage is occurring and can take steps to cut down on wastage or to improve production.

Bringing poor performers up to speed

The goal is 'to improve production' – but suppose there's an individual who isn't? Your team's performance needs monitoring as carefully as any other aspect of your project – particularly as your primary objective is to develop teamwork. How do you deal with the one who appears to be holding the rest back by not performing to standard?

First, it's important to define just where the performance is failing and how that failure is affecting the rest of the team. Is it holding back achievement of the critical path factors? Is work being produced on time but not up to standard? Is work having to be done over again, playing havoc not only with timing but with budgets as well? Is the failure one of behaviour or of productivity? Poor behaviour might manifest itself in interpersonal conflicts, lack of co-operation, failure to accept accountability, a tendency to blame other people, unacceptable attendance record, latecoming. Poor productivity might appear as producing work where the standard is not satisfactory, failure to produce to agreed deadlines, less work being produced than by others. Before you take the poor performer to task, it's appropriate to ask yourself some questions both about the person and about yourself as his or her manager.

1   Have you always noticed a slight drop in productivity when this person is introduced to a new task? If so, and the work always catches up to standard after a few days, then try to allow slightly longer deadlines, and cost accordingly.

2   Do you honestly believe this person capable of doing what you are asking? Don't confuse training with knowledge – just because something has been shown doesn't mean that it's been understood and absorbed. If, for example, he or she seems incapable of producing work on time, would it be better to move this person to another part of the project? Decisions have to be taken quickly – you can't afford to risk either the success of your project or that all-important team-knitting. I always think 'can't-dos' are a bigger problem than 'won't-dos; 'won't-dos' can be turned into 'will-dos'. 'Can't-dos' force you to make sometimes painful decisions – do you accept that the work currently being produced is of the highest standard possible for this person and accept that standard, with all the results that this might have on the rest of the team, or do you reluctantly admit that a square peg has been put into a round hole and decide that a replacement is necessary? If only I could find a clear-cut answer, I'd be a millionaire! Unfortunately, it's a decision no one can advise you on but it does need an objective look at how much of your management time you are spending on this person compared with the results that you can expect – difficult if you are a Feeler.

3   Are you sure you have not allowed a conflict situation to develop wherein this person feels isolated? It's very easy for the rest of the team to perceive that this person is letting them down and, unfortunately, the closer the team the more there can be a witch-hunt against the person who is not fitting in, for whatever reason. It is essential that grievances are listened to and acted upon quickly – I'm not talking about every whinge you overhear, but genuine grievances.

4   Are you sure that you are in no way contributing to the problem? Do you, for instance, only ever take notice of people who are not performing, on the basis that 'the good ones don't need motivation?' Are you giving feedback on the progress of the project? Have you been clear about the scope of the project and this person's role in the scheme of things?

Have you checked understanding? Are you showering with detail someone who simply wants to see the overall picture? When you need to criticize this person, are you carefully observing the five Ps of criticism?

The five Ps of criticism

Positive criticism should be:

- *Precise*: the person being criticized needs to know exactly where performance is failing and the standard to which you want it improved.
- *Polite*: if someone is aware of failing the rest of the team, the last thing that one needs is a bullying, disrespectful approach which will increase the vicious circle of poor performance, lowering of self-esteem, poor performance.
- *Private*: yes, we all know the old maxim 'Praise in public, criticize in private' but I can't be the only manager who has ever fallen down on this one; we are human, for heaven's sake!

  What I do think is important is that if we spill over into public criticism we also give the apology in public afterwards; again, I'm sure I'm not alone in having blown my top in public and then a little later called that person over to my desk to receive a quiet apology. The rest of the team, hearing the explosion but not my apology, gets the idea that it's OK to behave to people like this.
- *Performance-related*: it's perfectly OK to say to someone 'Your work needs to be brought up to the same standard as everyone else, and here's how you can close that performance gap'; however, to say: 'You're lazy and careless and you'd better pull your socks up' is not OK. Quite apart from being non-specific, it's just reinforcing that person's failure. What is needed is a picture in the mind of success, not of constant failure.
- *Posture-backed*: which really means controlling your body language, but that would have spoiled the alliteration! Unless your words are in agreement with what your body language

is saying, the body language will be believed every time. Thus to say 'The important thing is that your performance improve to this standard', while your body language is passive – smiling, avoiding eye-contact, hands to the face – carries the message: 'I'm not comfortable giving you this criticism and if things don't improve, then I'll just talk to you again in the same way.'

So, when you've asked yourself the questions and improved on anything in your own behaviour that you feel may be negatively affecting performance, what next? Now it's time to talk to the person concerned with the objective of bringing performance up to a standard which will contribute fully to teamworking and keep the project on track. You need to agree with the employee an improvement plan which is achievable and measurable. Explain exactly what the performance gap is between current performance and acceptable standard. Ask the employee why he/she thinks this is happening. Use the 'next-time' approach – 'this is what I want to happen' – rather than getting bogged down with what has gone wrong. Ensure the person concerned knows and understands the effect his/her non-performance is having on the team and the project. Ensure understanding by questioning, and make it clear that while you will, within reason, give advice and help, accountability for improvement is the employee's.

Remember, too, that it just might be a communication problem between yourself and the non-performer. Just as in England we assume that everyone can understand English if we shout loudly enough, not stopping to consider that if someone doesn't understand English they won't understand any the better for being shouted at, so some of us as managers think that the answer is to repeat exactly what we said last time but this time with an edge of irritation in the voice, not stopping to consider that perhaps a change of approach would be appropriate. Perhaps, of course, all that might be needed for the necessary improvement is someone *else* spending a hour with the poor performer. This is no reflection on your management skills – it's just that you may be approaching from a different personality, as we discussed in Chapter 2. You'll need the humility to accept that on this occasion, someone else can be more effective than you. Humility is not a virtue usually found in a list of desirable managerial characteristics – but sometimes it's essential.

Risk analysis

Involve your team in helping to assess risks to your project, using this sheet; then decide on strategies for dealing with high probability/ high impact risks and low probability/ high impact risks.

Risk	Likelihood	High/low Impact	Evasive/ remedial action

Improvement plan

Use this form to confirm a conversation with your poor performer, *never* to replace a conversation. Be realistic about improvement deadlines. Paint a specific picture of success.

Employee's name: **Date:**

Satisfactory performance will have been achieved when:

This can be achieved in the following stages:

By (date)   Improvement expected   Achieved

Are you contributing to poor performance?

This is for you to identify where your own management style might be contributing to an employee's poor performance. It will help you to decide where your own style needs to be adapted to accommodate differing people.

Do you:

Always   Usually   Sometimes   Never

Give adequate feedback?
Recognize achievement ?
Resolve conflicts?
Undersupervise?
Oversupervise?
Give effective performance
  reviews?
Ensure training for change?
Keep open communication
  channels?
Over-react to performance
  problems?
Refuse to delegate?
Over-delegate?
Criticize in private – praise
  in public?
Understand motivation?
Give mixed messages on
  quality and quantity?

5 Developing team communication skills

This chapter's objectives are:

1 To remind you of methods of communication and the skills required for those methods.
2 To help you make your project progress meetings more effective.
3 To identify the barriers to straightforward communication.
4 To help you to set limits by staying assertive.
5 To provide ways of persuading other people.
6 To give you the rules for negotiation.
7 To help you recognize 'communication games'.

All your careful planning and monitoring will be no use at all without successful communication. This seems so obvious that you may wonder why I bother to write it but it's amazing how little communication goes on in some so-called teams. Meetings are held where attendees leave at the end wondering what it was all about; individuals go off on their own kite-flying expeditions without feeling the need to liaise with anyone else; grievances boil up against the team leader but instead of getting things sorted out, team members whinge to each other; team leaders only really talk to team members to tell them that their

67

work is unsatisfactory, on the basis of 'you won't have to ask whether you're doing well – you'll soon know if you're not!'

Let's look first of all at *methods* of communication, and then we'll discuss communication *skills*.

Methods of communication

1   *Verbal*: quick, easy, but very open to misunderstanding, which can sometimes be deliberate. When you're communicating verbally, be sure to use terms which give no room for doubt, and to check understanding. Use vocabulary that is accessible to everyone – don't use technical terms to a non-technical person; he may understand anyway, but why take the risk?
2   *Hard copies*: essential when you need to be absolutely sure that information has been delivered and received. Particularly necessary when the information is complicated, or when there is a change in procedures.
3   *E-mail*: useful for immediate and/or simultaneous information. If the information is important as well as urgent, remember to follow up by hard copy. E-mail will be the death of communication, though, if we're not careful; there are companies where people who work in the same room, at adjacent desks, only talk to each other by e-mail.
4   *Individual communication*: can be used for coaching, and always to be used when you're dealing with a poor performer, or giving criticism.
5   *Small-group communication*: used to convey information or to solve a problem which is peculiar to just a few people. There is little point in a couple of people sitting through an entire meeting when only about one per cent of it concerns them – much better to meet with them separately. Small-group communication is also useful for some coaching situations.
6   *Full meetings*: these need to be explored in detail, so let's look at them closely.

Meetings

You may not be surprised to learn that when, on a training course, I ask managers for the biggest time-wasters they encounter, 'meetings' is always high on the list. They resent time spent in 'meetings for the sake of meetings' which never seem to lead anywhere, and where something that could be settled in ten minutes is allowed to drag on for hours. Let's look at some ideas for making your project progress meeting more effective.

Why are you meeting?

First – and I know this sounds obvious – know why you are calling the meeting. If you have little to discuss, would a memo or an e-mail be more efficient? Why does everyone have to be here – would it better to have just the couple of people directly concerned? You need to be able to complete the sentence: 'What I hope to achieve by this meeting is … '.

Who should be there?

Decide which people really need to be there. No one should be at the meeting if there is not an 80 per cent chance of their contributing, which means deciding whether some topics might be better dealt with at small-group meetings. Alternatively, deal with items of common interest at the beginning, so that those to whom the rest of the meeting does not apply can then leave.

Down with any other business

Probably the biggest time-waster at any meeting is 'Any Other Business'. I recommend that it never appears on your agenda! Instead, give everyone a date when agenda items must be in and make it clear that anything not on the agenda will not be discussed. If by chance someone tells you just before the start of the meeting that something important has come up which needs discussion, then tell everyone there is an extra agenda item. This is much better than allowing all sorts of trivia to be raised as any other business just when everyone thought the meeting was ending.

Timing the agenda

Talking of agendas, I find it very useful to have all items timed. If you have allowed, say, 20 minutes for a particular item and discussion has gone on now for 25, you are then justified in saying something like: 'We allowed 20 minutes for this and we're over-running; can we come to a decision, or shall we're-table it for the next meeting? And if we're re-scheduling, can we just agree on where we are so far?'

The preparation of the agenda is an important piece of planning, but need not necessarily be your job. Let everyone know who is responsible for it and the closing date, and leave it to other people. Do personally contact everyone who undertook something at the last meeting to be reviewed at this. It's better to take a minute to remind Mary or Paul that you will want to review progress than to spring it on them at the meeting and discover that it hasn't been done. Everyone is human – everyone forgets sometimes – everyone appreciates a reminder.

Start on time

Managers often ask: 'How can I make sure that the meeting starts on time?' I can only tell you what I do, and that is to start on time, even if only one other person is there. If people know you'll wait for them, there's no incentive to arrive punctually. The other thing I've found works is putting the most important items of the meeting at the beginning – and never repeating them for latecomers.

Encouraging contributions

It is important that the attendees have the opportunity to contribute and that no one is allowed to hog the floor. If you have people around the table who are reluctant to contribute, a good idea is to divide up into pairs or trios and ask them to come up with ideas on a particular point. It's quite difficult for two people to sit looking at each other in silence for five minutes. (Why do you think trainers are always splitting you into groups?) You may, of course, have people who give you the opposite problem – they want to take over the whole discussion. Try to avoid putting them down; if you do, other people will be reluctant to speak up in case the same thing happens to them. Instead, say something like: 'What do you, as a team, think about this point? Bill, I know you'll have some good ideas, so I'm going to save you till last.' Another thing you can do is to ask Bill to be responsible for recording proceedings, so that his attention is taken up with that. The person who gets the bit between his teeth and gallops off down byways can be interrupted when he stops for breath by: 'Bill, I appreciate your input but I'm not sure what it's saying to this particular agenda item; will you explain, please?' Some teams will take matters into their own hands, of course – I remember one training programme where I stopped to ask 'Any questions on that point?' and the delegates all broke into a chorus of 'Not you, Bill!'

Approaching problems positively

One of the phrases to avoid if at all possible at your meeting is the dreaded: 'We have a problem with ... '. For one thing, *we* don't have a problem – individuals each have part of the problem. For another thing, problems are powerful breeders and before you know it everyone is saying: 'Yes, that's a problem' and every suggestion is greeted by 'Yes, well, the problem with that is ... '. Here's the best way round that I know – and you'll have to take the lead yourself to set an example. Make it a ground-rule of your meetings that no one may say 'I have a problem'; people may only say 'I need to know how to ... '. Thus, instead of 'I'm having a problem getting people's reports in on time', you will have 'I need to know how to get people's reports in on time.' Everyone then brainstorms solutions, no matter how far-fetched, and from the list the speaker chooses one course of action that seems workable. Now, instead of everyone objecting 'But the problem with that is ... ', someone else may say: 'Well, if you're going to do that, then I need to know how ... '. In this way you're moving the problem-solving forward, everyone is looking for solutions instead of problems, people are taking accountability for setting their own part of the problem right, and an atmosphere of positivism instead of negativism is being created.

The action plan

As the meeting moves forward, instead of taking minutes (which next time will be read and no one will remember), why not create an action plan, like this:

Item Discussed	Action Agreed	Person Responsible	Start Date

This ensures a feeling of movement from the meeting instead of a static record of discussions, and the meeting has been a valuable investment of time. To ensure this, the think-sheets for this chapter contain a few reminders for meetings, whether you are chairing or have delegated the chair in order to be an attendee. Either way, you will need well-honed communication skills.

Communication skills

To be a good communicator, you need to be able to:

- give information clearly
- listen well
- set limits by staying assertive
- persuade other people
- negotiate to agreement
- cut through communication barriers.

We shall look at each of these skills in detail.

Communication should be easy – after all, one of the first things we learn to do is how to speak; unfortunately, we don't at the same time learn how to listen. Effective communication needs both skills from all parties involved, but so many things can get in the way.

Barriers to communication

1 *Lack of time*: we're busy people – we throw out a few words to someone as we go past – we tell ourselves we've communicated an idea; the person to whom we've spoken is having a bad day and perceives that we can't be bothered to stop and speak properly; communication has broken down.
2 *External noise*: especially if we're not really interested in what we're being told, or we don't really want to hear it, it's very easy to allow ourselves to be distracted.

3   *Misunderstanding of a situation*: your perception and mine may be very different. You may know that it is vital that we reach a certain stage in the project by the date set; I may have perceived it as a 'do your best' situation.

4   *Words used*: we have already discussed the importance of using words which are freely understandable to everyone. If I'm not awfully sure of the meaning of a word used, but everyone else seems to understand it, I may feel I'll look stupid if I have to ask for clarification. Keep it simple.

5   *History of relationships*: if in the past you've only acknowledged me when I do something wrong, then when you do finally say 'You've done a good job', my automatic reaction will be 'Oh yes, and what do you want?' I was once asked by a client company to spend some time with their training manager, whose training was perceived to be uninspiring, so that staff were not signing up for training programmes. After my first 'sit-in' on one of her sessions, I said to her, 'I really liked the way you approached XYZ topic – I've never looked at it from that angle.' She said glumly, 'BUT?' When I asked what she meant, she said, 'Well, whenever someone pays a compliment in this company, there's always a BUT … '. I thought it sad that when I said 'There's no BUT' she said 'Then why would you have bothered saying anything at all?'

6   *Our own backgrounds*: if this training manager had always received negative criticism at school then joined a company where that happened, it's not surprising that she would have taken for granted that all communication was going to be like that. Think back to when you were at school; in assembly the Head read out those dreaded words '[your name] will report to my office at break-time.' Was your first thought 'Oh good, I'm in for a pleasant surprise?' Since psychology tells us that all our lives we carry the child part of ourselves with us, it's not surprising that when you say to one of your team 'Will you come and see me at two o'clock so that I can check your progress' you get the reaction 'Now what's wrong?' If you just change the wording a little to: 'You seem to be making good progress with this – let's get together at two o'clock and discuss it', you've taken away a lot of possible resentment and defensiveness, which in turn

may lead to a conflict situation, with increasingly aggressive communication on both sides. You need an adult way of setting limits in communication for both yourself and other people – 'this is acceptable, this is not acceptable.'

Setting limits assertively

Aggressive people want above all else to be obeyed, in a lot of cases accompanied by a wish to be feared. There is no doubt at all that they often get their way – people will do as they are told. However, it's a short-term success because it arouses resentment and people will not buy in; indeed, they will often find ways subtly to sabotage things. If we're treated like children, we tend to behave like children. The limits set by aggressive people therefore get blurred at the edges.

Passive people, on the other hand, are desperate to be liked, and they will agree to almost anything in order for that to happen. They appear to perceive that they have no right to set limits for themselves, while accepting that it's perfectly proper for other people to do so. They find it very difficult to say no, with the result that they often take on too much, and nothing gets done properly.

Effective setting of limits needs a different approach, one which accepts that I not only have rights but that with those rights come responsibilities. If, for instance, I have a right to be treated with respect, then I have a responsibility to treat everyone else with respect. So when limits are set, the setter is clear and honest about the way he or she chooses to be treated. Here are some helpful phrases for various situations.

To avoid lengthy disagreements
'That may be so; however … '.
'I'm not disagreeing; however … '.
'I hear what you're saying; however … '.

For example:

A team member: 'To do what you're asking will mean working two hours overtime.'
You: 'I hear what you're saying, however, it's necessary if we're to keep the project on track.'

This approach will not make the person concerned like you, but it shows respect, it says you have listened, and it indicates that you are not about to get bogged down in who is in the right – you are willing to stick to what is necessary. However, there are times when you have taken the wrong decision or made a mistake, when it would sound flip to use this technique. Honest apology is necessary without encouraging finger-pointing.

To acknowledge your own mistakes
Appropriate phrases here are:

'I'm not surprised you're mad – it was the wrong decision; I apologize and I suggest that now ... '.
'If you'd forgotten to do that, I'd be as mad as you are with me. I apologize and I will ... '.
'You've every right to be angry; I apologize and I'll put it right by ... '.

Note that you're not drowning in self-recrimination; you're simply accepting accountability for your behaviour and its results and you're taking what steps you can to put things right. This approach worked for me with a traffic warden in Southampton – he was so taken aback when I said 'You're quite right to give me a ticket – I shouldn't have parked here', that he let me off! I can't guarantee that this would always be the result in this situation, and I haven't pushed my luck since!

To avoid getting into a defensive argument
One more technique before we leave limit-setting: some phrases that can be used in the face of attack such as 'You *never* seem to', 'You *always* seem to ... ', 'We're not getting *any* back-up from you ... ', when we are all apt to become aggressive in defence are:

'Tell me specifically when this has happened.'
'Give me an example.'
'Tell me specifically what you would like me to do and I'll tell you what I can commit to.'

As with so many other situations in life, 'it ain't what you say it's the way that you say it'. Watch that your tone doesn't become sarcastic or threatening or the other person's whole perception of what you say will change, and he/she will become much less amenable to persuasion.

Persuading other people

How do you persuade people to do what you want them to do without a four-act drama every time? There are four main ways of persuading people – telling, selling, wheeling and dealing.

1 *Telling*: there is no doubt that sometimes telling is necessary; you can't take time to wheedle your way through every request you make. Health and safety, for instance, is an occasion where action has to be taken now. Save it, though, for occasions which really need it and never accompany it by threats such as 'This needs to be done by Thursday and if you can't do it there are millions of unemployed who can.'
2 *Selling*: the golden rules in selling are: 'Sell the benefits' and 'Use the you-factor'. If you can present genuine benefits to the team or individual from following your ideas, you're much more likely to get buy-in. If you can use the word 'you' more often than 'I', as long as it's being done positively, your suggestion will have more appeal – in other words, this is what it will mean to you, rather than this is what I want you to do.
3 *Wheeling*: this is really manipulation, and manipulation doesn't have to be negative. Quite often you can use a leading question to 'wheel' someone to a situation where you can sell your idea to them: 'If there were a way of doing things which would make life easier, save time and trouble and produce good results, would you like to hear about it?'
4 *Dealing*: this is the negotiation situation, and since negotiation is a very important part of the communication in a project, we need to look at it more closely.

Negotiation

The whole basis of negotiation is an exchange of wants and benefits. If it is to end successfully it will require compromise. If neither party is prepared to move then stalemate results, and the negotiation is null and void. The operative words are *if* and *then* – 'If you will do this now, then I'll make sure that someone else does it next time.' 'I can certainly do that, if you will do this'. This 'iffing and thenning' means that you take a step towards each other all the time until you meet – not necessarily in the middle but at a place where you both feel you've got a good deal. Some rules to observe when negotiating are:

1   *Co-operate, don't compete.* In a tug-of-war, one team may pull the other over the line, but you're all flat in the mud. So it is in negotiation – you'll get much further in a three-legged race, where either both win or neither does. So ...
2   *Aim for a win/win result.* As long as you both have what you wanted at the end, it really doesn't matter if the other party perceives that he/she has won. In fact, a lot of negotiations are ruined by failure on one or both parts to stick to rule 3.
3   *Keep your ego under control.* It's very easy, especially if you don't feel particularly friendly towards the other person, to get to the stage where you are determined not to give in; you see his point of view, you know that the compromise would work – but you're not going to let him win. When this happens, remember ...
4   *Don't win a battle but lose a war!* The trouble is in so many negotiations that we forget about tomorrow, when we shall have to work with the other person. If one side gets its way over the other, all that happens is that an atmosphere of resentment is created, and any further negotiation necessary will be approached with defensiveness.
5   *Honesty is the best policy.* You can lie like a hairy egg in any negotiation situation – once. The other side will never trust you again. Presenting a situation honestly means that decisions can be made based on the facts as they are, with no room for later recriminations.
6   *Remember your own objective.* You started this negotiation in order to achieve agreement, not to prove the other person wrong.
7   *Try to get their whole wish-list.* If you start agreeing concessions before you know everything the other person wants, you're in danger of being 'sliced'. Don't agree to anything until you've asked 'Anything else?' and noted it all down. Then you can start your if-and-then: 'I can certainly agree to that, but only if you ... '.

A successful negotiation will move everything forward while keeping team relationships intact – it's worth approaching with care.

Watch out for flying pigs with this next statement: 'if you adapt all the approaches we've discussed so far, all your team communication will be straightforward sweetness and light.' Of course it won't, for the simple reason that everyone – you and me included – plays communication games from time to time. Let's look at some of them.

Games people play

'Why Don't You – Ah Yes But'

The commonest communication game we all play is 'Why Don't You – Ah Yes But'. (The names for these games were invented by Dr Eric Berne, who identified the whole concept of game-playing as part of his work on transactional analysis. They are now universally accepted.) In the game mentioned, one person presents a problem, and the other suggests a solution; the first then finds a reason why that won't work (Ah Yes But). The second suggests another solution and the process continues until the second person runs out of suggestions. The first player is thus confirmed in the belief that this situation is quite beyond control and that he or she cannot be blamed for anything! This game can be interrupted right at the start by the second person, instead of offering a solution, offering options: 'You could do this, or this, or this – which do you think you'll do?' If there is a reason why none of these would work, then pass the ball back: 'OK – what do you suggest?' If someone is constantly reluctant to make decisions without consultation, just check to see that you are not over-supervising; it just might be that you are giving out the message: 'I'll make the decisions around here.' Ask yourself, too, how you deal with mistakes – if people find their heads shot off every time they make a mistake, they will be very reluctant to act unilaterally.

'Do Me Something'

Another very common communication game takes the form of 'Do Me Something'. This is also known as 'Pass the Monkey'! Person A says: 'I have a problem, and you must sort it out for me.' Person B, pushed for time, uses those four fatal words in any manager's vocabulary: 'Leave it with me.' Person A goes off happily. Person B either finds a solution ('heals the monkey') in which case it's no more than Person A expected – it's part of Person B's job; or he fails to find a solution and the monkey dies, in which case it's confirmed that the manager isn't as clever as he thought he was! Refuse to accept monkeys! The reason why we use the 'leave it with me' phrase so often is that it takes time to help people feed their own monkey, and time is something we never seem to have enough of. However, if by sitting down with the person and asking: 'What do you think you can do about this?', even if it takes half an hour for them to identify a solution, you're going to ensure that you don't get that particular monkey again thus it's time well spent. The other important point is that your people will never learn to solve their own problems if you are always willing to solve them for them; you'll be helping them to develop by passing the monkey back to them.

'Havoc'

In 'Havoc', someone in the team that is working well and whose project is progressing favourably starts to complain about something. At first, no one takes any notice, but it's insidious and people start to think that yes, perhaps that ought to be put right, it really is not good enough; before long, what was a well-motivated team is turning into a team of whingers. Clamp down on 'Havoc' as soon as it starts, by asking: 'What can we do about this? Nothing? OK – do you feel so strongly about it that you'd like to join another team? Or come off the project?'

'Let's You and Him Fight'

This is another trouble-making game. Person A complains to Person B about Person C's behaviour/ performance/ lack of co-operation, 'but don't say I said anything'. Person B tackles Person C, without mentioning Person A's complaint; bad relationships develop between Persons B and C, while Person A is able to stay lily-white and clean, possibly even agreeing with Person C in private that it's a bit much. My suggestion is that if Person A has a complaint about someone else in the team, she deals with it.

'Ain't It Awful!'

Then, of course, there is not a person alive who has not at some time played 'Ain't It Awful!' Isn't the company awful, the job awful, the manager awful, the project awful? Some teams will even tell you that things are better after what I once heard described as a 'Whine and Jeez' session – they say it clears the air. It doesn't – whinges breed prolifically. I recommend that as soon as you hear this game, you come in again with that question: 'What can we do about it?' The answer is usually nothing, so let's get on with the job. I believe very firmly that it's essential to have a 'whinge in your own time' rule, because you'll never get the best out of a team of 'Ain't It Awful' players. After all, if the company and everything connected with it are rubbish, what kind of rubbish must we be to work here? You don't get the best out of rubbish. The very best way I've found to deal with this is to ask at a meeting: 'What kind of team do we want to be perceived as by the rest of the company? By our project sponsor? Most importantly, by ourselves?' If this sounds a bit 'touchy-feely', I can only say that I've used this with very un-touchy-feely salespeople and later with managers, and it has worked well. If I had ever had a team who said 'We don't care a fig what the rest of the company thinks about us', I'd have had to consider very seriously whether I wanted to carry on leading them or look for another job! When the whingeing starts, instead of coming down heavily you can just say 'We wanted to see ourselves as a team who got on with the job, didn't talk behind each other's backs, got differences out of the way. We need to see how we can get back on course to that.'

Open, honest communication can make the difference between your project's achieving your prime goal of building better teamwork and finishing up with people who are demotivated and demoralized. There will be times when your project is not going as well as you would like it to, and your communication will have to be slanted towards motivating people to get it back on track without apportioning blame. This is what we shall deal with in the next chapter.

Reminders for meetings

Use this as a tick-sheet and analyse your own performance after your next meeting.

If you are chairing:

Note what you want this meeting to achieve
Plan how you will recognize achievements since last meeting
Check with those responsible for action points
Set the agenda close date
Compile and distribute agenda
Stick to your timed agenda
Control discussion
End motivationally
Circulate action points after the meeting
Action your own commitments

If you are an attendee:

Check your commitments from previous meeting
Submit agenda items on time
Prepare progress report on your part of the project
Be on time
Keep contributions concise
Stay assertive, not aggressive
Listen as well as talk
Carry out your commitments as soon as possible

What is your natural persuasion style?

This questionnaire is devised to be used with your team members, either at a team meeting or with them filling it in on their own for discussion afterwards. Point out that this will show their natural, preferred way of persuading people and that if they seldom get the reaction they hope for, a change of style may be appropriate. We tend to fall into our natural style particularly when we are tired or harried, so they – and you – need to be especially alert at these times.

You have ten points to distribute among the parts of each answer – for instance, in question 1, if you would be most likely to give response (a), then you might give that 6; if (d) would be your next most likely, you might give it 3; (c) might rate a 2; and perhaps you would never say (b), so you'd give it 0. Please don't mark according to what you would like to say, or what you think you ought to say – the whole point of this is to identify your own usual persuasion style and consider if on occasions you would get a more positive response by changing a little. On the answer sheets, put your mark for each answer and then total up the columns. (A word of warning – the letters on the answer sheet are not in alphabetical order. I merely point this out, since sometimes delegates get halfway through and then find they have misread it.)

1   One of your peers is very fond of chatting, which plays havoc with your time control. You've put up with it up until now because you know he lives alone and gets lonely, but now it really has to stop. Do you say:
   (a)   I must get on now, but let's have coffee together.
   (b)   I'm sorry – I've no time to talk.
   (c)   If we meet up at lunch-time, we'll have more time to talk.
   (d)   Wouldn't you rather talk in comfort over lunch?

2   The leader of another team is being difficult about giving the co-operation you need to facilitate your project. Do you say:
   (a)   That's how it's going to be – if you don't like it, tough!

Reproduced from *Developing Teams Through Project-Based Learning*,
Jean Atkinson, Gower, Aldershot, 2001.

(b)   If you thought this would be good for both our departments, would you change your mind?

(c)   The report to the MD will of course give credit to your department.

(d)   This project will be of benefit to customer care in both our departments.

3   One of your team is affecting everyone by constant negative comments. Do you say:

(a)   The atmosphere will be so much better for everyone if you stop this.

(b)   Stop this, or I'll make it a disciplinary matter.

(c)   You can feel as negative as you like – just keep your views to yourself in working hours.

(d)   Are you feeling so negative that you'd rather be working for someone else?

4   One of the team is reluctant to accept responsibility for part of the project, though you know it's well within her capabilities. Do you say:

(a)   OK – if you won't do that part, then you'll just have to accept whatever's left.

(b)   Tough! You'll do as you're told!

(c)   I believe that success in this will count favourably towards your promotion.

(d)   I don't want to have you do a more difficult part, but I'll have to if you won't accept this.

5   Your team feels slightly threatened when you introduce new charts for monitoring project progress. Do you say:

(a)   If you thought they were going to make life easier, how would you feel?

(b)   By using these, we can be sure we won't have to catch up with a lot of slippage at the end.

(c)   These are professionally accepted ways of monitoring any project.

(d)   We'll use them for a month; if you're still unhappy, we'll see how we need to adjust them to make things easier.

6   One of your staff has been on an advanced IT course, and her understanding of IT is now above that of her colleagues.

Reproduced from *Developing Teams Through Project-Based Learning*,
Jean Atkinson, Gower, Aldershot, 2001.

She is reluctant to share that knowledge, saying that it is quicker to do things herself. You suspect that this is in fact an ego-boost for her. Do you say:

(a)   Would you rather share the knowledge or personally refund the cost of your course?

(b)   You were sent on the programme specifically so that you could teach the others.

(c)   I believe you enjoyed that course – there's no point in sending you on another unless you share knowledge.

(d)   By sharing your knowledge with other people, you get to stay on the project team.

7   Your accounts department is slow in paying invoices, and one of your suppliers is threatening to stop supplies. Do you say to the accounts manager:

(a)   Is there any way we can get the supplier to change the way he sends invoices, so that payment could be expedited?

(b)   I'm going to have to take this to the MD.

(c)   Once this is sorted out, it will save both of us so many hassles.

(d)   If we can sort this out now, it will save having to bother the MD.

8   Your team will have to work a little late to bring the project back on track, and your company does not pay overtime. Do you say:

(a)   If everyone works till six tomorrow evening, we shall have an easier life over the rest of the project.

(b)   I'm sorry – I'm afraid we'll all have to work late tomorrow.

(c)   There's one way we can catch up and stop the hassle – shall I tell you?

(d)   If everyone will work over tomorrow, we can all finish a little earlier on Friday.

Persuasion style score sheet

NB: the answers are not in alphabetical order – for instance, number one is set out b, c, d, a. I merely point this out because people don't always notice, and get very cross when they discover it!

Reproduced from *Developing Teams Through Project-Based Learning*, Jean Atkinson, Gower, Aldershot, 2001.

1	b	c	d	a
2	a	d	b	c
3	b	a	d	c
4	b	c	d	a
5	c	b	a	d
6	b	d	c	a
7	b	c	a	d
8	b	a	c	d

telling	selling	wheeling	dealing

6 Developing rescue skills

This chapter's objectives are:

1 To help you identify reasons why your project may be going off-course.
2 To give you some ideas on rescuing a project from time slippage, including managing your own time.
3 To provide you with ideas on intervening in the stress cycle that is likely to arise from project slippage.
4 To provide ideas on maintaining effective leadership during difficulties
5 To offer ways of tackling conflicts which may arise during the project's rescue.
6 To help you make decisions on the future of the project.

If you follow all the advice and suggestions given up to now, your project will sail through without a hitch – whoops, there flies another pig! Almost all projects meet hiccups – major or minor – sometime in their life-span, which have to be overcome if the project is going to come home with the three sides of its triangle intact, plus a motivated team. Most teams will pull together well when they're on a high because success is in sight – it's when the whole thing starts to look doubtful that your powers of leadership and development will have to come to the fore.

Possible reasons for project slippage

The great advantage of the charts we discussed in Chapter 4 is that you can see immediately if things start getting behind. Fall down on your monitoring, and you could be several days adrift before you realize it. There is no doubt that *lack of planning* and *'what-iffing'* at the start are responsible for most project breakdowns, but there are of course others. If the project is a long-term one, *motivation* may run out of steam; some team-members may start to *'fly their own kites'*, adding in their own ideas without reference to anyone else; *insufficient communication* may result in a lack of interest and this may well result in sniping and *conflict* within the team, as well as slippage on the project itself. Remedial action will have to ensure that your prime objective of team development gets back on track, as well as getting the project back where it should be, and should concentrate on rescuing the project, not on allocating blame. There are some blame cultures in which the ongoing feeling is 'someone will get me if I fail, so I won't report mistakes or slippage, I'll just hope it comes right in the end; and I'd better not ask for help, or they'll think I can't hack it.' Employees in this culture have both fear of failure and anger at the system bubbling very near the surface, and since it's not OK to lose their temper with management they are looking all the time for someone else to blame for their failures. The culture becomes one of 'I'm not OK – you're not OK'; 'I'm not getting the result I want and it must be your fault'. This is why all through the book we're discussing the importance of the next-time approach – 'how can we put things right?'

In the case of a project which starts to lag behind, one side of the triangle will almost certainly have to be adjusted, if only temporarily; maybe you'll have to throw money at it for a very short while, which means planning to recoup it further down the line. If you have done an assessment of risk before you started, you'll be in a better position to weather the storm. You may even have to do some paper borrowing from one part of the project to help out another, but you can't do this too often! Therefore, keep a close eye on 'creeping cost' over-runs and make each team member conscious of and accountable for that part of the project. Introducing changes into the original plan is almost always costly, another reason for careful thought at the start and for watching out for 'kite-flying'. Beware, too, of the IT maniac who is constantly going 'back to the drawing board' on computer to come up with better ideas via computer-aided designs. There comes a time when, even if a better way is discovered halfway through the project, the cost of change would outweigh any benefits.

Organizing your time

What about time slippage? Again, your charts will be your bibles. Critical factors become top priority, especially when costly slippage starts to appear. It is here that your handling of poor performers becomes important, especially the can't-dos – it may well be that parts of the project have to be re-assigned in order to catch up. This, of course, is a good reason not to be talked into a project where resources are so small that they will be stretched to the limit – your won't-dos have you by the ears if they know they are irreplaceable.

Your own time management will need to be absolutely on the ball if you are going to carry out your own share of the project plus monitor everyone else's progress, plus do any of your own usual work which might be running alongside the project. Time management is a very personal thing, and really consists of recognizing priorities and ensuring that they are done first – our critical factors. I believe that if you are in control of 60 per cent of your work-day you are doing well, when you allow for all the reactive tasks which come up every day in the course of work. I've read the books, too, which say you should be able to account for every minute of your time and not allow yourself to be sidetracked by interruptions, but I don't know where these writers live – certainly not in any organization I've ever worked in! Those of us who teach time management have no more reason to be smug than anyone else – it's just that we've learned the hard way that if you work for clients you can't afford not to be organized over your time. The main difference between someone who finishes the day frazzled, with nothing done, and someone who finishes frazzled but with a sense of achievement is that the latter knows what hasn't been done, so can plan tomorrow. That person has also learned to build uncommitted time into the time-plan, so that one emergency doesn't mess up the whole week.

The reason that so many of us have problems with time management is that (a) we're not sure of priorities in the first place and (b) we allow ourselves and others to believe that we are superhuman and can juggle twenty priorities at a time, with one hand tied behind our backs, while cracking walnuts with our teeth. In fact, even a Flyer (remember Chapter 2?) will juggle ten things at once but must prioritize in order to have a hope of finishing the important ones.

The first rule, then, for controlling your time is to know what your goals are – in your case to develop teamwork by successfully carrying through this project. The second is to keep in mind the key result areas (KRAs) of your job; in most managers' cases these are staff control, budget control, self-development and productivity; in your case now, you'll have added another – project management. You may, of course, perceive that your own KRAs are quite different from these – it doesn't matter, the principle stays the same. It is unlikely that you'll be able to spend the same length of time in any week or month on each of your KRAs; last month you may have concentrated nearly all your time on the project, while other areas of your job took a back seat. This next month, therefore, you may plan to spend more time with your people, making sure that they are performing well, plus finding time to read a book for your own development.

Once you have a rough idea of where you want your time to go over the next month, you can draw up your weekly time-plan. *Set as priorities this month the Critical Factors of your project*, then sketch in the things you know are due this month – staff review, monthly management meeting, and so on. Ensure that your weekly list contains some uncommitted time – not free time, you understand, just an hour here and there when you will have time to discuss problems, deal with unexpected emergencies, check the progress of your project. Very few emergencies can't wait for half a day, until your uncommitted time comes up – after all, what would happen if you were away at a meeting? Thus your whole week won't be thrown out of kilter because your boss calls an unexpected meeting – you have some uncommitted time in which to do what you had planned for that meeting time. Indeed, if you give your boss a copy of your monthly/weekly plan, it may well mean that his/her planning has to improve to fit.

Your *daily to-do list* can be compiled once you know your overall priorities; don't worry that you'll have so much free time you won't know what to do with it! Work planned doesn't mean less work – simply that you're dealing with it proactively as far as possible. A word of warning about to-do lists: if you're not careful, they grow so long that they're meaningless. At the end of one day, you put anything you haven't got done on tomorrow's list; then, because it's not high priority it carries over to day three – along with things left over from day two. Before you know it, you have a list so long that it daunts you just to look at it, and you decide that time control is impossible. My advice is to put a limit on the number of times you transfer something; with me, it's three days, but for you it may have to be longer. If it hasn't been done within a reasonable time it's almost certainly for one of three reasons: it's not important, in which case stop carrying it over; you don't know how to do it, in which case ask for help; or you really don't want to do it, in which case, the bad news is that it's not going to disappear of its own accord. Either do it, or delegate it to someone else.

The reason why these lists grow so unmanageable is that we won't accept that if we have a full day planned, and something else comes up, it needs to replace something already on the list, not be added to it. It's a good idea, when you make out your list, to indicate roughly how long you expect that task to take; quite often, when you do this, you find that you have ten hours of work planned – and you only work an eight-hour day. Write this in letters of blood on your left forearm, where you can see it: 'I am not superman or superwoman; I can do most things, but I cannot do everything at once!'

Ideas to stop yourself going mad
Let me share some ideas that help me:

1　*Maintain a 'to-do list'* as we've already discussed.
2　*Stop buying-in to interruptions.* If you always greet visitors with 'No, of course you're not disturbing me' then you have only yourself to blame if they take you at your word.

 The most effective way I know is to stand up as the interrupter comes in, especially if you say something like: 'I'm up to my neck now, but I've got some time about two this afternoon – can we meet up then?' I know that telephone interruptions are more difficult, but how about asking the telephonist to tell people that you are unavailable and will call back at a specific time? I know all the arguments against this: suppose it's an irate customer, suppose one of your team needs you – what would they do if you were out of the office? If the caller is given a specific time for you to ring back, this means that you can bunch your telephone calls so that they become proactive instead of reactive, and you can prepare for some of them before you pick up the phone.

3　*Use surgery hours.* If it's possible to set aside two or maybe three half-hours a day, when people know that your door is open and you are available, they will learn to make their own decisions between those times. Of course there will always be exceptions in emergencies, but this has been a life-saver to me. It is a wonderful encouragement to people to feed their own monkeys!

4　*Remember MBWA:* Management By Walking About is not only the only way to spot potential problems as they arise, it's also an opportunity to have a word now which may save you an interruption later. A delegate told me that he has taken to getting in before his staff, meeting them as they come in, and asking 'Anything we need to talk about today?' A positive response results in a time being set for a meeting, so that now he has 'interruptions by appointment'.

5　*Learn to delegate.* Of course it takes longer to show someone else how to do it than to do it yourself – once. But if you show something which will then be taken off your hands for the duration of the project, then that seems to me a very worthwhile investment of time. The only thing to remember is that the person to whom you delegate it may not do it as you would – try not to interfere as long as the results are the standard you want.

6   *Plan as far ahead as possible.* Some things – meetings, performance reviews, for instance – occur regularly throughout the year; they can be planned for well in advance so that the rest of your time is built around these non-negotiables. If you're a Flyer, you will get a great sense of virtue out of seeing things planned so far ahead!

7   *Control paperwork – or it will control you!* There was a time when we were promised the paperless office – what went wrong? Project progress reports, memos, trade magazines, letters from customers, scraps of paper with messages to self written on them – so many of which are filed away 'just in case'! What I rely on is 'the five Ds of paperwork': do it, defer it, delegate it, divert it, dump it (I know that in these environment-conscious times I should say recycle it rather than dump it, but that would spoil the alliteration.)

- *Do it*: take some action, if it's only to put it into an 'Action this day' folder. I have a friend who keeps a folder marked: 'Too difficult to deal with today'. Needless to say, by the end of the week, the folder is bulging and – surprise! – the tasks in there have not got easier! I do not recommend this approach! I too have read the books that say 'Pick up each piece of paper only once'; I believe that to be excellent advice, but I can't make it work. What I do do these days, though, is to put a small dot in the corner of any piece I pick up; pretty soon, I realize I'm spending more time picking it up, dotting it and putting it down than it would take to action it. I was giving this advice on a management programme when a delegate said: 'I do something even more effective; when I pick up a piece of paper tear a tiny piece off the corner – if I don't action it soon, there won't be any left!'

- *Defer it*: this is perfectly acceptable as long as you do it positively, and don't just pick up the paper, look at it despairingly and put it down again. I promise you this idea works: have six manila folders piled in a tray on your desk and mark them Monday, Tuesday, Wednesday, Thursday, Friday and Action This Day. Anything urgent goes into the last-named, anything non-urgent goes into the appropriate folders for the days when you have scheduled uncommitted time. You then have to commit yourself to actioning it on that day – not looking at it and then putting it into yet another folder! Be realistic therefore about your time availability – no point in deferring everything into Thursday's folder, or you'll be back where you started. Is some of the paperwork non-urgent enough to go into one of next week's folders? I'm sure there are more sophisticated systems, but this one works for me; it's cheap, simple, and the pile of folders in my tray is difficult to ignore.

- *Delegate it*: let the team know who is in future responsible for collecting these papers, and make sure you monitor on a regular basis. One word of warning – do you remember how you felt when you were a team member and you suspected that you were giving information to a secretary or colleague that your manager never saw; you thought what a waste of your time it was. It's important, therefore, to allow yourself time to read, comment and take action on these returns on a regular basis.

- *Divert it*: this is a variation of the last idea. Is it really necessary for you to see all this paperwork? For instance, if you never seem to get time to read the trade magazine, and you're afraid you may be missing information on developments within the industry, can you get someone to precis articles for you? Or can you start a company library where these magazines are kept for reference?

- *Dump it*: while I was writing this, I suddenly realized that my way of dumping is in fact recycling. You may well gasp in horror at what I'm going to suggest here; if so, you can go on amassing so much paper that you spend ages looking for something when you need it. Did you know that researchers have discovered that 87 per cent of paperwork which is carefully filed away is never referred to again? Of course there are a few things which you know must be kept, and a lot which you know you need not keep. It's the ones you're not sure of that you're apt to keep 'just in case'. These are the ones this system is designed for.

Here's my patent recycling method, which I learned some years ago and which works beautifully. You need two ordinary A4 envelopes; put them in the top drawer of your desk. When you're not sure whether or not something is important enough to save, don't waste time looking at it and wondering – put it into one of the envelopes. After a while – about three months in my case, but maybe longer or shorter in yours – the envelope will be full. Seal it down, and start the other one. When the second is full, take the first one to the recycling bin *without opening it*, or shred it and then recycle it. The not opening it is important – if you do, you'll get cold feet. Before you throw up your hands in horror, think this through. That envelope has been there now for six months and you haven't needed anything in it, so how likely is it that you're ever going to need it? If by chance you get a phone-call saying that you haven't actioned a memo, then you can get a copy from a Regulator who has saved everything. (That's after you've tried what we all do by reflex – deny ever having received it!!) If all else fails, you ring to say you can't seem to lay your hands on it and can you have a copy. It may seem drastic but you've got to find time from somewhere to rescue this project without stressing out yourself and everyone else in the team. When stress levels rise, tempers fray and teamwork is eroded.

Dealing with stress during the rescue

Stress is not the same thing as being busy. You can dash around like a mad thing all day, or drive long distances, and be very tired at the end of it but not feel stressed. Stress arises when a combination of physiological and psychological factors convince us that we are out of control; not 'a great deal of work', but 'more work than it's possible to achieve in the time available', not short deadlines, but impossibly tight deadlines. It's our mind and body warning us that we are setting ourselves impossible targets. We start to feel like victims, with no one to rescue us. Our perception on the situation becomes skewed – we start to use more 'absolutes' in our conversations – 'I *always* do that', 'I'll *never* get done in time', '*Everyone* will think I can't hack it', '*No one* but me gives a hang'. We start to pile work on to other people, causing our stress to spread to them. A vicious circle is set up, but it's interesting that this circle doesn't start with stress at all – it starts with perception, thus: perception of things going wrong → stress → perception that things are worsening → more stress → darkening perception → burnout if the cycle is not interrupted.

To take an example: you have an awful lot of work to do to rescue the project; your perception is that it's impossible, which not unnaturally causes stress; stress causes you to lose a little confidence in yourself, and you perceive that if this project is not delivered satisfactorily you will be seen as a failure. The stress of this keeps you awake at night worrying, so next day your powers of thinking and rational decision-making are blunted; things seem even more out of control, with deeper stress resulting. You just *know* – here you go, thinking in absolutes – that your promotion prospects will be affected by failure with this project; you are now getting stressed out of your mind! You start to take your stress out on the team, who resent this and unite against you – you are even more a victim. You perceive that you will probably lose your job over this, your partner will leave you, you will have no money, you will finish up walking the streets with all your worldly belongings in a supermarket trolley! Fortunately, before this happens you have a breakdown, and are led away to lie down in a darkened room. This increases your stress enormously – now it must be obvious to everyone you can't cope – they'll probably keep you on but with no responsibility, probably cleaning the washrooms ...

Can you see how it is perceptions that are causing the problem here? These are what we need to challenge right at the beginning, to put ourselves back in control of the situation.

Fortunately, we can interrupt this cycle at any stage by simply changing our perceptions – note that I say this is simple, not necessarily easy. When the project looks as though it's impossible to salvage, instead of perceiving disaster, ask yourself which of the project triangle's sides need to be adjusted to make it salvageable. Then talk to the team or to your sponsor about adjusting the time or cost – or even the quality. You are now taking charge of things. If you are told that the time is non-negotiable and the budget is tight as it is, then use the 'I need to know how to ... ' approach by throwing the ball back in their court: 'You're quite right to be frustrated, and I accept accountability for underestimating at the start. Would you like us to abort the project, or do you think there will be a little more money in the budget?' They may well want to get into the 'This shouldn't have happened in the first place' mode, in which case you can say 'That's absolutely true – however, what we're trying to do now is to salvage the project – that is unless you'd prefer us to abort?' You're no longer the victim; you're back on an Adult to Adult basis.

When you start thinking later on that this will affect your promotion prospects, catch yourself up and ask yourself: 'So?' Turn the nightmare scenario into a question to yourself: 'If there will not be promotion for me here, what will I do? Will I stay anyway, because by and large I enjoy this organization, or will I keep an eye open and, when it suits me, leave?' You're back in control of your own life and the stress is receding. I know that some of you are saying: 'But my boss will say "No excuses – it's got to be done on time and within budget"'; if this were possible, you would already be doing it. Pass the ball back. If you truly feel that this has damaged your standing in the company, then again take a decision about your own future. Deciding not to decide is a decision – you might tell yourself 'I'll do nothing for six months, then I'll re-evaluate the situation and decide whether to stay or go.' Each decision takes the stress level down a little further.

Signs and symptoms of stress

The most important thing to accept about your stress is that it is *your* stress and you are the only person who can really deal with it. Similarly you can't lift other people's stress for them, although as you are team leader, your team has a right to expect that you not add to it. You need to be aware of symptoms in yourself and signs in other people. Symptoms you may experience may include:

- *Loss of appetite* or conversely a need for comfort-eating. A lot of people eat more when they are stressed – it's one way of taking decisions for yourself. Just remember to say: 'I choose to overeat at the moment – it's a comfort thing' rather than 'I just can't stop eating' when you are perceiving that even food in the fridge is more in control than you are. Is there a worse victimhood than being victim to a packet of crisps?
- *Difficulty in sleeping* or the reverse – your subconscious mind knows that it's not going to able to cope today so says 'Let's not wake up'.
- *A need – as opposed to a liking! – for alcohol.* If you always go to the pub at lunchtime with the team, you're friendly, not stressed; if you absolutely could not get through the day without that drink at lunchtime, stress is there.
- *Loss of libido*: of course we all get headaches occasionally, but if you know that in a contest between your fantasy partner and a crossword, the crossword would win, you're probably stressed.
- *Any change of habit* – heavier smoking or starting smoking, drugs of any kind from a craving for coffee to happy pills to something stronger, if it's something you don't usually do and are becoming addicted to, identify what it is that's stressing you. If you've always been snappish with everyone, you're not stressed, you're just a miserable blighter; but if you're usually easygoing and you're now at the stage where people are frightened to talk to you, look out.

Look out for similar signs in your team members, including uncharacteristic carelessness at work or performance problems. Over recent years, employees have been awarded large damages from their companies because they have claimed that their jobs were causing stress, so quite apart from the good of the project, it's in your interest to intervene in someone's stress cycle if you can. This is not always easy in a project where resources of every sort are tight, including staff, but it's better to delay the project by a day or so now, or to take on a little extra work yourself, than to finish up way off course because a key person has to have a long spell off.

How do you tackle a situation where someone tells you that a situation outside work is causing so much stress that it is affecting performance? The golden rule really is not to give advice – just listen and help to recognize options. Point out that the team is relying on this person. If there is pressure outside work, then at least you can make sure that worries are not added to at work by performance slipping. You might also give him/her a copy of the 'If you're feeling stressed can you … ' questions at the end of this chapter.

Remember, too, the old saying that 'if you carry on doing what you've always done, you'll carry on getting the results you've always had'. If you've been successful up to now, don't change a thing; but since we're talking here about rescuing yourself from stress and the project from slippage, it might be appropriate to look at different ways of doing things, even if that means challenging existing beliefs.

Leading through difficult times

Survival experts say that when disaster hits a group of people – fire, flood, shipwreck, plane crash – the leader has to ensure that certain actions are carried out in a specific order if they are to survive. Hopefully, disaster has not hit your project, but the ideas hold good, I believe, whenever people are looking for leadership in a difficult situation, and your project showing slippage is certainly that. Let's look at their advice, and how it refers to your project.

1   *Calm things down.* Don't look for people to blame; hide the anxiety which you will quite naturally be feeling yourself; discourage negativism; avoid panic decisions.
2   *Provide shelter.* This is probably the most difficult thing for any team leader when the going gets tough. Every part of that project is your accountability, no matter to whom you've devolved it, and the team has a right to expect that, whatever you say to them in private, you will defend them to senior management or to the project sponsor. 'I take accountability, and I will make it sure it's put right.'
3   *Signal for help.* There is nothing 'macho' – in either gender – in struggling along trying to put the project back on course

by yourself if there are people whom you can consult for help. Take suggestions from your team first of all – just because you're the leader, no one should expect you to have the monopoly on ideas. If they have nothing new to offer, seek advice, first of all from people who have done similar projects and then from your own managers. Remember that part of your boss's salary is paid to make sure you succeed and develop in your job. Here's an interesting fact: psychological research shows that of every hundred people you know, ten are expected to help you no matter what (family, partners, close friends); ten would not spit on you if you were on fire; and the remaining eighty would willingly help if only they knew you needed help. (Yes, I too wondered what sort of questions researchers asked to compile this information.) That's a lot of help you may be ignoring!

4   *Ration resources.* You're doing this all the time with your charts and CPA, rationing time and money. Incidentally, the experts say that, contrary to what you'll see in adventure films, in a survival situation most of the water should be drunk at the start of the operation, since you need to be fully hydrated to make rational decisions; they say you can survive at least three days without water – you won't be in very good shape, but you can survive. (You're going to thank me for all this when your balloon crashes in the jungle.) This says to me not that you need to use all your budgetary resources at the beginning of the project but that we need constantly to question accepted beliefs, especially about what is and isn't possible.

5   *Avoid dangerous actions.* Dangerous actions which may destroy teamwork and sabotage your project will be those we've mentioned – panicking, blaming, failure to defend your team, failure to monitor progress – and failure to resolve conflict.

Resolving conflict

It's amazing how many people are reluctant to invite confrontation, never mind deal with conflict. You and your employees have only so much time and energy. Every bit of each they spend on arguing and sniping is one bit less of each they have to spend on helping to rescue the project. Whether the conflict is between two members or between a team member and yourself, it needs to be confronted and resolved. If you have a difference of opinion with a member of your team, the first thing to take on board is that that person may just be right! We've all seen the notice in some offices: 'Rule One – The manager is always right; Rule Two – If the manager is wrong, Rule One still applies.' Unfortunately this is how it really is in a lot of teams – especially if things are not going well with the project and the manager perceives criticism where in fact just another point of view is being presented. Therefore the best way I know of approaching a potential conflict situation is to ask three questions:

1   Why are you telling me this?
2   Why is this important to you?
3   What would you like me to do?

The answer to this last question may well be something like: 'We should never have tackled it that way in the first place', in which case your reply is 'That may well be true, but what do you want me to do about it now?' You work with adults, and adults accept the fact that it's no good throwing all your toys out of the cot because you don't always get your own way, so you won't always be able to follow suggestions as to what he/she would like you to do – indeed, to do exactly as suggested in some cases would be anatomically impossible and very dangerous! However, instead of retorting 'You've got more chance of being torpedoed on a motorway', or something equally managerial, explore the other person's wishes. 'What would be the positive outcome of that?' 'What might that affect negatively?' 'Will you do some costing on time/money on that idea?' Yes, I know this takes more time than a snappy answer – that's why you've left yourself unallocated time on your time-plan, and if it gets this issue resolved instead of constantly recurring, isn't that a good investment of time? Of course there are times when you have simply to say, 'No, I can't do that because … ' but the more you empower the person to consider his own suggestions, the better for team harmony.

If the conflict is a really serious one, and relations look like breaking down, then sit down with the person concerned and say something like 'We're never going to agree on this particular point, so let's work on something we can agree on. What is there that we both want? OK – the team working together and the project back on track. Our arguments are affecting the team's working together, so they have to stop. We both want the project back on track – let's agree to bury our differences until that happens. We can always come back to them afterwards, by which time they may appear easier to solve.' There has to be some want you both have in common, or why on earth is this person still on the team? Find it and work towards it.

Suppose the conflict is not with you, but between two team members? The first thing to identify is whether and how the argument is affecting teamwork and the rescue of the project. If everyone knows that John and Pauline just don't get on, but that's OK – work carries on smoothly round them, then it's probably no concern of yours anyway. They may just enjoy hating each other. If work is going well, meetings are not disrupted by their mutual dislike, the team functions well, then let them get on with it – just make the rule 'hate each other in your own time, not the company's'. If, however, as so often becomes the case, their dislike is affecting progress of the project, as mini-teams start to form behind each one, then you will need to take some action. I've tried two ways of doing this – both have proved successful on different occasions.

1   Sit down with the warring parties and take the tack that I have suggested above – find out their common needs or requirements. 'I want her to stop ... ' 'Well, I want him to stop ... ' are not common requirements! If this is the dialogue that's forthcoming, then feed them with 'do you both want this project to succeed?' 'Do you both want us working as a team?' If the answer to either is 'I don't really care', then get that person off the project at once if at all possible, even if it means redistributing workloads. Once you get a positive answer, encourage exploration of that: 'John, what will you do to ensure this?' 'Pauline – what do you need to stop doing – no, not what does John need to do – but *you*?' Don't expect an outpouring of repentance! However, if you make

it plain that you are insisting on an answer, it will eventually come – grudgingly, reluctantly, but it will come. They will never be friends, they dislike each other as much as ever, but remember you are not talking about their attitude, only their behaviour.

2   A couple of times I've simply said to the parties concerned, 'I'm going to leave you here in my office for thirty minutes. At the end of that time please have your differences resolved at least to the point where you agree to stop sniping at each other.' I do know it seems unlikely that grown men and women will respond to this, but you have to remember that it is not the Adult part of them that's behaving this way – it's the child in them. You might want to try the second approach first, so that you can get on with things while it's going on, and if there is not a satisfactory conclusion then move on to the first.

Making decisions

Decisions about conflict-handling are important, and are only part of the decisions you have to make if the project is going off-course. There is a great temptation to be panicked into one of two courses of action, particularly if this is a team-generated project rather than one reporting to a sponsor. You'll be tempted either to turn a blind eye to problems, and go blithely forward getting further and further off-course, or to decide that everything is more trouble than it's worth and abort the project. If it's team-generated, remember you've set the goal-posts, you can move them; you can adjust the sides of that project triangle as much as you like as long as teamwork is holding good throughout the changes. It's obviously going to be demotivating for everyone, especially 'Here and Nows' and Regulators, if you're constantly changing, so that people don't know where they are; but a meeting where you discuss with the team how the project is slipping and how it can be saved, particularly if you take their suggestions on board, can increase the feeling of all pulling together.

If you are carrying out this project for a sponsor, either another manager or department or an outside sponsor, then of course discussion with that sponsor must take place. Be very honest about what has slipped and why, and your proposals for getting back on track. Have this discussion as soon as you perceive difficulties – it won't get any easier for leaving it! Have some suggestions ready for each of the triangle sides. Can you see a way of making up time-slippage later in the project, and on what are you basing your hopes? How will this affect the sponsor's plans, and how can you help to minimize any effect? If you change specifications, will this help make up the time, and how happy will the sponsor be with these changes? If you assign extra staff to the project, how will that affect the outcome? Who will bear the extra costs? Remember that the sponsor will not be delighted with you anyway – she will be even more angry if you simply go in with a list of problems which you seem to expect her to solve. Much better to approach with: 'I suggest that we do this and this, if your budget will stand the extra sums involved; or if money is an issue, then we can stick to the agreed budget by making a small change to specifications here, which will not affect the overall quality, or by rearranging delivery times. Can we discuss which of these would cause you least hassle?'

However your project is generated, you will need to decide by discussion with your team:

- *Do we continue or abort the project?* How much time has been spent on it? How much money? How long will it take to get back on course? Will this be worthwhile?
- *How will team spirit be affected if we abort?* How will it affect the way we approach future projects? How will we feel about ourselves?
- *Given the position, what are the risks in continuing?* Will they outweigh the advantages of continuing?
- *Can we pinpoint the causes of delays or overspending?* If you can't identify where and when things started to go wrong, still without allocating blame, then you're unlikely to be able to rescue the project. If the main cause seems to be your own failure to monitor closely enough, then say so and ask for suggestions.
- *Are we enough in control to rescue things?* Or are things happening which are quite outside our control – a flu

epidemic, a strike at a supplier's? We said earlier that while risk assessment is vital before you begin, you can't allow for every single possibility; have you been overtaken by events?

- *Are we approaching these questions objectively*? If you have invested a lot of team time and effort in the project, are you looking objectively at the probable outcome if you continue or if you abort?

One way of clarifying your thinking is to do what in salesperson's terms is known as the 'Duke of Wellington Close'. It is said that the Duke of Wellington, before he took a major decision about a battle, would divide a piece of paper in half lengthways, and then mark one half 'plus' and the other 'minus'. This story is probably apocryphal, especially as it has also been attributed to Napoleon and Winston Churchill, but it's certainly a good way of clearing your mind. All reasons for a decision go under the plus, all those against it go under the minus, and then you tot up. You may, of course, find something on one side which outweighs almost everything on the other – 'ruining team harmony' on the negative side, for instance, might mean that you decide to abort.

You will of course have to negotiate around these points with a sponsor. It may be that you will have to write a full report, or do a formal presentation on progress so far and why the project needs extra resources. You may, indeed, have to do either or both of these if the project is brought in successfully, so the next thing we consider will be verbal and written presentation skills.

Are you stressed?

First of all use this form for yourself, to identify your own stress levels; then let your team members work through it. Always use this form in conjunction with the next one, 'Tackling stress'.

Always   Sometimes   Rarely   Never

Do you feel irritable and behave accordingly?

Do you have difficulty in sleeping?

Do you have difficulty in facing the day?

Is your concentration slipping?

Are you making careless mistakes at work?

Have you lost enthusiasm for everything?

Have you lost your appetite?

Do you overeat?

Do you feel you just can't cope?

Is decision-making difficult?

Is the world out to get you?

Is your energy level low?

Do you need alcohol to get through the day?

Do you find it difficult to relax?

If the answer to all the above is never, take your pulse immediately because you're probably dead!

If the answer to all of them is always, do not slit your wrists until you have turned to the next think-sheet for suggestions on how to relieve stress.

Tackling stress by making changes

At work, can you:

Set yourself more realistic objectives?
Refuse nightmare scenarios?
Get to the office a little earlier?
Cut down on taking work home?
Develop assertiveness, rather than aggression or passivity?
Give yourself more credit?
Ask for help when necessary?
Plan your time more effectively?
Delegate more?
Plan some uncommitted time?
Be strict about carry-over items on your 'to-do' lists?
Improve your self-talk?
Learn to watch out for stress symptoms?
Learn to interrupt the stress cycle?
Learn to say: 'So what?'
Accept that work is an important part of your life – it's *not* your life?

Outside work can you:

Talk less about work?
Have at least one non-work-related hobby?
Pay your bills, so you'll be broke, but not stressed?
Leave your computer occasionally?

Project rescue sheet

Ask each member of your team to complete this individually. Then encourage all team members to discuss their ideas at a team meeting and from these compile an action-plan, which, remember, may be that you have no option but to abort the project.

1   Our project has slipped at the following points:
     (a)   Budget: estimated:
                    actual:

     (b)   Time-scale: estimated:
                    actual:

     (c)   Quality specifications: agreed:
                    achieved:

2   These slippages have occurred because of:
     (a)   Factors inside our control:

     (b)   Factors outside our control:

3   Slippage can be corrected by:
     (a)   Work re-allocation:

Reproduced from *Developing Teams Through Project-Based Learning*,
Jean Atkinson, Gower, Aldershot, 2001.

(b)   Agreeing new time-scales:

(c)   Assigning more staff:

(d)   Agreeing new budgets:

(e)   Working overtime to get back on track:

(f)   Agreeing changes to quality specifications:

Our team values

Discuss these values with your team before the project starts. You will almost certainly be surprised at how the team is perceived differently by different team members. Use this sheet to redirect behaviour if tempers get frayed because of the project's slippage.

As a team, we work together well.

What is important to us is getting things put right.

We work on discovering what went wrong, not on who went wrong.

We accept that it's OK to ask for help.

We sort out differences within the team, never washing our linen in public.

We remember all the time that the team will be here when the project is finished.

7 Developing presentation skills

The objectives of this chapter are:

1 To give guidance on the production of written reports and verbal presentations.
2 To clarify rules on grammar.
3 To help you structure your report or presentation.
4 To guide you on the use of visual aids.
5 To suggest ways of your using body language and voice effectively.

It may be that your project is designed to be of interest only to your own team. It is more likely, however, that at its conclusion – or indeed at stages of its progress – you will have to inform someone else of results. It may be a sponsor; it may be that your project has shown results which the rest of your own organization will benefit from; it may be that you know you will be looking for further funding for future projects, so that you are anxious that this one be widely seen to be successful. Whatever the reason, you will want to present as professionally as you can so that the presentation becomes part of your successful project; and a presentation is certainly an opportunity to develop teamwork still further, as different people undertake writing and proof-reading for written reports and different sections of a verbal report. In some cases, the sponsor may want both a verbal presentation and a written one – maybe in order to study results at leisure, having had the opportunity to ask questions.

Remember always that your own prime objective in this project was to use it to develop teamworking. Group presentations are an excellent vehicle for this. Not everyone will be happy standing up to present; these can be a support service for those who will. Overheads may have to be produced, charts and tables prepared. The presentation in itself becomes a mini-project within a project, with its own Gantt chart and CPA. The rule is never, ever, to throw away any paperwork at all arising from the project – even those dimensions sketched on the back of an envelope may later be developed to form part of your report and/or recommendations. Save absolutely everything – in an old A4 envelope is fine – until you are quite sure that the project is completed and your presentation is ready.

Written reports

We're going to look at written reports first of all. It's a proven fact that a three-page report takes about five hours to prepare. If you are going to invest this kind of time, you want to know that your report will not only be read, but acted upon, so it's worth making it as easy to read as you can.

Getting started

Unless you are very unlike most of us, the sight of a blank sheet of paper, or an equally blank computer screen immediately brings on a burning need to do something else – phone a colleague, check the office temperature, feed the cat, drink a cup of coffee – anything! The best way I know round this mental block is simply to write – anything remotely connected with the subject – just to overcome the expectant gaze of paper or screen. I work on the 'get it down and then get it right' principle; it's much easier to correct something already written than to write it in the first place. The introduction, therefore, might be the last thing you write – we'll see in a moment that the same thing applies to a

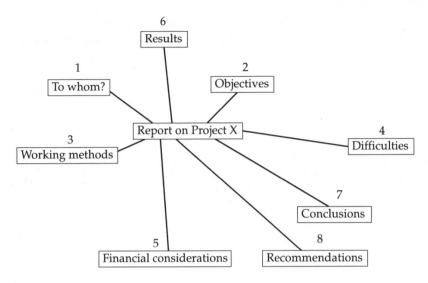

Figure 7.1   Getting started on a written report: an 'exploded diagram'

verbal presentation. You may or may not find useful the sort of 'exploded diagram' I always use to design courses, prepare reports, or anything which needs sequential setting out (Figure 7.1). You will see that what I've done is a kind of personal brainstorming. There's no attempt to get things into any kind of order at first – just jot down anything as it comes into your head. Then you can decide on a logical sequence, and number your 'branches' accordingly.

This approach is now generally known as mind-mapping, although I find the term 'exploded diagram' more graphic. Each heading may of course have further branches – for example, branching out from 'working methods' you may well have 'people involved', 'training provided', 'resources used'; when you come to write up your report, each of these can have a separate section or it will simply remind you to include these details in your writing.

Introduction
So, you have your headings in front of you; the page is no longer accusingly blank; you're in writing mode. The introduction, which as we've discussed may in fact be the last thing you write, needs to explain the rationale behind the project:

This project was undertaken to discover why so many customers are appearing on our credit blacklist. We allowed 28 days for the project, which had to be carried out in conjunction with our normal working, and we estimated that the cost would be limited to phone calls and, in some cases, working time to visit the clients.

This, as you see, sets out your project triangle against which to evaluate success. Time: 28 days; cost: phone calls and visits; quality: information gathered. For your own project, your estimated costs may have been quite considerable and your time-scale much longer, but the same reason for this introduction applies. Actually, in view of the fact that your prime objective in all this is to develop teamwork, it may well be that you can devise a project which costs virtually nothing but may have important impact.

Paragraphing

Remember that each new topic needs a new heading and each new thought needs a new paragraph. Paragraphing is particularly important in a long report. New paragraphs give people permission to stop and take a breather, thus avoiding the 'oh-good-grief-I-can't-tackle-all-this-now' feeling on the part of the reader. A few link-phrases are good for introducing paragraphs: 'So much for … , now … '; 'Having looked at … we come to … ' ; 'Because … , the next step had to be … ' and so on. These help the report to flow freely, taking the readers' thoughts along with it. However, a report is not a novel, so resist the temptation to strew it with adjectives and flowery phrases.

Grammar

I have spent some time wondering whether to include the next few points; I am well aware that a lot of people worry over correct grammar, especially if they came through school at a time when grammar was considered old hat. You will want your report to convey the best impression possible, so let's look at a few basic grammar rules. If grammar has never been a headache for you, go on to the next section!

Punctuation

Full stops are no problem – everyone knows that at the end of a sentence you need a full stop. However, if you have too many short sentences in a row, your report will start to sound staccato; you need something to break up your sentences, while separating the thoughts – either a *comma* or a *semi-colon*. If you've never been sure of the difference, don't worry too much about it – you could get through the rest of your life without ever using a semi-colon if you had to. However, they are very useful in separating complementary thoughts whilst also helping to vary sentence lengths. The rule is really that if you just want your reader to stop and take a short breath, you use a comma, as you see after 'breath' and 'comma' in this sentence; if a slightly longer pause is needed, use a semi-colon, as after 'sentence' here. The semi-colon indicates that we are still continuing the same train of thought, but you might want to pause for a moment here. The colon (:) is usually used to indicate that either a list or a quotation is coming next, and in these cases nothing else will really do.

Inverted commas – or quotation marks – can be confusing, since rules are changing. You may have been taught to use double quotation marks always for direct speech. This has changed, and it's now perfectly acceptable to use single quotation marks everywhere; you will find that single marks are used nearly everywhere in this book, for instance. However, problems arise when there is a quotation within a quotation. If we have a sentence such as 'John said, "This is not going to work"', the use of double quotation marks for John's words tells the reader that this is a quotation within a quotation, and in fact you will be very glad to have the facility of two sorts of inverted commas here.

Something I'm often asked is: 'Should question marks and exclamation marks go inside or outside the inverted commas?' That depends on whether or not the question/exclamation is part of what's in the quotation or not. A couple of examples:

'Have you read "The Eagle Has Landed"?'

The question mark comes outside the quotation marks, because the book is not called 'The Eagle Has Landed?' – you are simply asking the question. However, it would come inside in the following example, because it is part of the title being quoted:

'I have just read: "Who Killed Kennedy?"'

At all costs try to avoid sentences like :

At this point, John asked: 'Are we calling this project,
"Will We Ever Finish?"?'

Two question marks because John is asking a question, and he is quoting a potential title which is itself a question. That way madness lies – you'd do better to say: At this point, John asked whether we should call the project 'Will We Ever Finish?'

Two other questions people ask a lot: 'Does the *apostrophe* go inside or outside the S?' and 'How do you know whether to write "it's" or "its"?' If this is something you've never been sure of, it's because when you were at school, teachers would tell you that the apostrophe denotes ownership; so you wrote 'The dog wagged it's tail' because the dog has ownership of the tail. You were marked wrong, at which point you decided that grammar was for the birds!

Now – forget everything you ever learned about ownership in this context; an apostrophe has one meaning only – it means *something has been missed out*. Long, long ago, in ye olde English, no one would say: 'This is Robin's cup'; they would have said 'This is Robin – his cup'. You can see the same thing if you look in parish records for your family history. Until universal education, a lot of people couldn't write their names, so would sign a document with a cross, and the witness would write 'John Brown – his mark'. Eventually, everyday speech would run the words together – 'This is Robins cup'. No problem as long as communication was verbal, but once written communication became common, there had to be some way of indicating that this should really be 'Robin – his cup', so the apostrophe was born to show that the 'hi' had been left out of 'his'. (Very educational, isn't it? Aren't you glad you bought the book?) So, to know on which side of the 'S' the apostrophe should go, just ask yourself what has been left out. If you are saying

'This is the boy's train',

you're replacing the 'hi' from 'his' with an apostrophe. If you are wanting to say that several boys are playing with the train,

'This is the boys – their train',

you're missing out the whole word 'their', so that's where the apostrophe goes:

'This is the boys' train.'

So in your report, you might say something like:

'John's hard work paid off' (John – his work)

or

'The employees' efforts were rewarded'
(the employees – their efforts)

Once you've grasped this idea, you never have problems again with 'its and it's', because you just ask yourself whether something is missed out. 'It's a nice day' should be 'it is'; the 'i' is missed out so it needs an apostrophe; 'the project was now drawing to its successful conclusion' – here nothing is missed out of 'its', so no apostrophe needed. And in case you're wondering why, if all this be so, we don't say, 'This is Mary's book', having missed out the 'he' in 'her', it's because in the days of ye olde English, women were not regarded as owning anything – the very dress a women wore was regarded as the property of her nearest male relative – so there was no point in devising an abbreviation for a concept that did not exist.

Who or whom? gave me hassle for years before I devised a way of remembering the rules. Do you have trouble knowing when to use 'who' and when to use 'whom'? I would too if I didn't use my patent way of remembering: just ask yourself, 'If I were not using either word, would I say I or me, he or she, they or them?' For instance, 'To whom shall I give this?' would be replaced by ' Shall I give this to him', not 'to he'. 'I shall tell this to whomever is in the meeting' would be replaced by 'I shall tell them if they are in the meeting', not 'I shall tell they'. All very well – so how do you remember? Easy – the word 'whom' contains an 'm'; so do the words ' me', 'him', and 'them'; 'her' goes along with him.

So, if you would replace the 'who' or 'whom,' by:

me
him/her
them
us

then you need 'whom'; and the only one you have to remember is 'us', since all the others contain an 'm'.

If you would replace the 'who' or 'whom' by;

I
you
he/she
we
they

then you need 'who', and you don't have to remember anything, just that they don't have an 'm'.

Structuring your report

If your project has been a major one and your report will be read by several people, you can make life easier for the readers in two ways: give each separate topic – the headings on your exploded diagram – a page to itself, so that the person to whom this is not relevant doesn't have to plough through pages of information to find it; and give a summary of your report right at the beginning before the introduction. Always include a contents page, even if your report is only two pages long; your reader will be much more kindly disposed towards you if he/ she can go straight to the parts of interest.

Active or passive voice?

You are also more likely to keep interest if you phrase your report, as far as possible, in the active, rather than the passive voice. Your grammar check will tell you 'this is in the passive voice', but never tells you what that means. The *active* voice is *direct*, moves the action along, is usually more concise: ' John undertook this part of the project', 'Mary helped Paul to collate the findings', 'We found that … '. The *passive* voice, on the other hand, is *indirect*, usually longer, more tedious, slows down the action: 'This part of the project was undertaken by John', 'Paul was helped by Mary to collate the findings', 'It was found that …'. I have to say then whenever I hear or read something like: 'It has been decided that', 'It will be appreciated if', my reflex response is always 'by whom?' This is not the response you want to evoke in your readers, so in most cases the active voice is the more appropriate.

Tables, figures, etc.

If you have a report involving tables or figures or technical specifications, it's a good idea to attach these as appendices. This means that people to whom they are of no interest don't have the flow of their reading interrupted, while people to whom they are important are directed to them by: 'See table at Appendix 3'.

Proof-reading

Your report is finished. You have your heading on a separate page, 'Report on a Project to … '; your contents page is clear; headings, sub-headings and paragraphs invite reading; your appendices clarify things even further. Can you now distribute it? No – not until you have checked and re-checked. Of course you have run it through the spell-check, but the spell-check is not infallible – it would, for instance, pass a sentence saying: 'Wee shell revue this two sea watt happens'! So it's worth proof-reading really thoroughly, or better still getting at least one other person to proof-read for you; if you can get someone to do it who has no knowledge of your project at all, so much the better – that person is more likely to be able to put on the reader's shoes (or reader's glasses, perhaps?). At the very worst, try to get it checked by someone who has not typed it.

Above all, we keep coming back to the fact that this project is to develop teamwork. Let each member of the team contribute ideas to the report and do be sure that they are familiar with its contents before they are questioned about it by the people who receive it.

Verbal presentations

A lot of what we have said about reports applies too to verbal presentations; they need to be clear, concise, with each point signposted with link statements, like paragraphing, to ensure smooth movement from one point to another. You have the advantage, though, of being able to back up what you say with body language, and the disadvantage that it's very easy to allow yourself to be led off down sideroads.

We'll look at a formal presentation to management or to sponsors, which you can adapt or scale down if you're talking to just a couple of people. We might divide it up under four headings – Plan, Practice, Present, Plan Further. Let's consider each of these in turn.

Plan

Your presentation's success will depend to a very large extent on how well you have done this stage. Decide what you will say, how you will say it, who will say it – and how you will stop. It has been said that a presentation is like a love affair – anyone can start one but you need a lot of skill to end one! It will be a great pity if your well-received presentation is allowed just to dwindle away at the end.

Assembling contents

What will you say, first of all? You will find the exploding diagram as useful here as for a written report – it will give you the points you need to cover and the order in which you want to cover them. It is at this stage, too, that you will get out that (by now very tatty) envelope into which you put all the paperwork arising from the project, shake them all out, and throw some of them away. What's left will reinforce your ideas and remind you of important points when you come to compile your notes. It's a very brave speaker indeed who gets up to speak without notes. However well you know your subject, however familiar you are with the topic, don't risk it. Here is a cautionary tale. One awful day, when I was a trainer with Yellow Pages, my mind went totally blank covering a topic I had covered literally dozens of times before. I was talking to a class of inductees about one group of customers who respond to advertising, known as NEDICT customers. I explained that N is for newcomers to an area who have not yet identified suppliers, the E is for people buying in an emergency, the D is for – and my mind went totally blank! 'The D is for … ', I repeated desperately, then 'But why am I doing all the work? What do you think the D is for?' (typical trainer's trick?). 'Desperate?' came an answer. 'No'. 'Desirous?' – 'No' – panic is setting in. 'Dissatisfied with their current supplier?' 'Correct!' I said, weak with relief. It taught me a lesson – always have notes! (In case you are wondering, the rest of that memory-jogger is I – infrequent buyers, C – competitive, just ringing round for quotes, T – transitory buyers, just passing through.)

Organizing your notes

So, if we agree that notes are essential, is there a best way of organizing them? You can, of course, simply write everything out word for word on A4 sheets. The danger here is twofold: (a) you'll be tempted simply read it out, thus losing eye contact with your audience and (b) if you do look up, it's very easy to lose your place. One way which avoids both these is to use prompt-cards – it will take you a little while to get used to them, but soon you won't want to use anything else. Don't, though, simply write out everything on the cards, or you'll have the same temptation to read. Your cards really need to look like this:

MAIN POINT

Development point
Development point
Development point

The main point on each card is the one on which this whole section of the presentation depends, while the development points are memory-joggers to help develop that point. If you plan to use any visual aids, you can indicate these in red, to the right of the card, and a number can go in the top corner. Keep your development points to not more than four on a card. Your card might read:

> CUSTOMERS ON BLACKLIST   3
> FOR A NUMBER OF REASONS
>
> Refusal to pay
> Cash-flow problems
> Delay in issuing credit notes
> Last one commonest

You develop each point as you go through, and the main point for development on your next card may well be: DELAY IN ISSUING CREDIT NOTES, with some points about this topic following. You will find that each card will hold about three minutes worth of talk. Time-planning is very important, of course. Very few people object to a presentation which is slightly shorter than allowed for, but they may well object to ten minutes over.

Maintaining interest
You will need to build 'interest peaks' in as part of your preparation. People's powers of concentration wane very quickly even if they are interested in the subject. Plan, therefore, to have something to change the energy – an overhead transparency, perhaps, or use of the flip-chart, or an unexpected fact, or a short anecdote about a happening during the project. Another way of focusing attention is to involve more than one person in the presentation, so that people have a change of voice.

Practice
Handovers, in fact, are something which need to be included in the second P – Practice. Wherever possible, rehearse aloud, even if you are on your own, because timing will be different when speaking aloud than when you're reading through to yourself. It is absolutely vital that, if you have to dovetail in with other people, you have rehearsed altogether, not simply having looked

at notes and having said, 'OK, I come in there.' Discuss, too, what questions may be expected, who will answer them and what the answer will be. Know who is going to use what piece of equipment and ensure that you both know how to use it. If you possibly can, get into the presentation room in time to check equipment before you start.

Visual aids

Use of visual aids is an important part of your presentation – as we have discussed, they're a good way to change the energy. A lot of presentations today are done from *laptop* to screen, ensuring very professional-looking images. Whether your own company does this or uses the overhead projector, do remember to look at your audience while you're talking, not at the screen. If you need to point something out, do so and then come back to your audience – it's very easy just to stand reading the screen, with your head turned away from your audience.

Your *overhead transparency* – always computer-produced, of course, even if you don't use the laptop to present – should be a springboard for your points, or a development of these; it's never acceptable simply to put up a sheet of close printing taken straight from the computer or photocopied from a book. If you need your audience to have this kind of information, give it in the form of a separate hand-out, and remember in your planning to build in time for people to examine them. Plan, too, whether you will invite questions as they read them, or whether you will ask them to leave questions till the end.

The *flip-chart* is the visual aid which you will almost certainly use during your presentation. This is still, to my mind, the most valuable aid of the lot. You can prepare it beforehand, as you can with overhead transparencies, but with the added advantage that you know the bulb is not going to blow. You can even prepare something which you would rather like to give the impression of having carried in your head – for instance, suppose you think the financial person in your audience would be quite impressed by your remembering costs of raw materials, before the audience arrives write up this information lightly in pencil on either the first or the last page of your flip-chart, so that you will know which page to turn to. Only you will be able to see it there, so when you say 'A few costs for you to consider' and proceed to write up these costs, following your pencilled notes, the impression will be 'This person's really on the ball'.

One more practical point about the flip-chart – I know it sounds obvious, but it's something I've fallen down on sometimes – do remember to try out your pens beforehand. It can be extremely disconcerting to try to write up an important point with a pen that won't write.

We've discussed the importance of not talking to the screen – the same applies to the flip-chart, because keeping eye contact with the audience is so important. If you're writing up a point, either stop talking, write it up and then discuss it, or talk about it first and then stop talking while you write it up – don't talk and write at the same time. If all your audience sees is the side of your head, you'd have been as well to send a written report, so ensure that not only do you look at people, but that you spread your eye contact round the group, thus avoiding impaling one person with your eyes.

Body language

A word or two about other aspects of body language: despite what a lot of people say, I think one hand in the pocket if you are a man is OK – but two hands in the pocket looks slovenly. On the subject of hands, if you can manage to keep them still and look natural, so much the better; otherwise concentrate on making them say what you want them to say. Held up in front of you, palms pointing to the audience, fingers slightly spread, says 'I won't discuss that – be quiet.' Held up, palms facing you, fingers slightly curving towards you, says 'Come along with me on this'. Try not to put your hands behind your back – you'll look as though you are going to 'tell people what' – and never cross your arms – you'll look like a dictator.

It's important to remember that no matter how experienced you are, you will almost certainly have a slight nervousness before a presentation, especially an important one, and that this nervous energy has to come out somewhere, either via your hands, your feet or your voice. Therefore, the best you can hope for is to channel this energy into movements which are not irritating for your audience – if you need to move your feet, for instance, move purposefully towards the flip-chart and back, don't stand in one place constantly shifting your weight from one leg to the other, or stand cross-legged, portraying your nervousness to your audience.

Voice

It goes without saying that this will be enthusiastic, but be aware too of speed and volume. Remember that a loud voice is not necessarily a clear one, so concentrate on clarity. This can often be affected by the speed of your delivery. It's perfectly natural that if you feel nervous, you tend to speak more quickly; this is probably something to do with the subconscious saying 'Let's hurry up and get this over'. If you normally speak fairly quickly, you will feel as though you are really dragging your words if you slow down a little; this is not so – you're merely using a speed with which your audience is comfortable. Changing speed as you go along can be a very good way of emphasizing a point; you're talking at a comfortable speed, you slow down to cover a really important point, you pick up speed again. Another way to stress something important is to pause very slightly before and after the point; if your audience's attention has started to wander, that very slight pause will refocus them.

Beginning and ending

These are very important parts of your presentation. Don't spend five minutes at the beginning assuring your audience that you know how busy they are and you will not take up too much of their valuable time! There are one or two ways to make your beginning interesting.

You can start with a *fact*:

'Six months ago, we wondered whether ... ; we are here today to show just how successfully this has been proved possible ... '.

You can start with a *question*:

'What happens if you take six people, give them a task which looks extremely difficult, and tell them that it has to be accomplished in six months?'

but if you do this, be sure you don't pause for breath at the end – pass very swiftly on before anyone can answer; an answer at this point can be very disconcerting!

Try to avoid the 'title' introduction – 'we are here today to discuss the success of this project' – people know that – it's why they've come.

Make sure you *set the scene* at the beginning, too:

'I'm sure that as we go along you will have questions; I suggest you make a note of them so that we can discuss them at the end – this will be more time-effective for you than bringing them in as we go through.'

Remember that the five decision-making motives still apply – have you found something about your project which will appeal to their financial, safety, comfort and ego motives, and are you presenting it in such a way as to cover that greatest motivator: appeal?

Remember, too, that the end is an important part of your presentation; simply to end rather feebly with 'Well, that's all I've got to say, ladies and gentlemen – thank you for listening to me' doesn't constitute an inspiring ending. Now it's quite safe to leave a *question* hanging:

'So, I would ask you – just how important is safety?'

Or you can tie the ending back to the beginning:

'Six months ago we wondered whether … I hope we've shown that not only has this proved possible, but that it's been extremely successful.'

If you can devise a strong ending, save it till after you have answered questions; you want this to be what the audience carry away with them.

Plan further

You need to do a positive post-mortem after your presentation – pick out what went well and decide how you will build on these next time. Don't let yourself get bogged down in: 'Oh good grief

– I shouldn't have said that there'. Ask yourself instead: 'If we could do it again, what would we change?' Think back to the points at which interest really seemed to spark – what did you say that caused that to happen? Give yourself credit for your good tactics and learn from your mistakes.

It really is worth giving some care to the way you present your project's findings. After all, it's very nearly the last stage of any project. Only very nearly? Well, there is one other important stage ...

Exercise

The following exercise would make a useful training session at a team meeting, as you approach the 'report' stage of your project. Divide your team into pairs or trios, and ask them to rewrite the report together. Because the report is not clear, and needs work to clarify it, it is a good example of how a piece of writing can appear perfectly clear to the writer, but can be more trouble to the reader than she is prepared to take.

Rewrite this report so that it is concise, readable and comprehensible. Remember the summary and contents page.

Report on costs of new washroom equipment

We examined the facilities at site A first of all and found that the washrooms there are on alternate floors, Ladies and Mens. We had suggested a few weeks before to the staff committee that the equipment in some of the washrooms throughout our site needed replacing, and other people agreed for their own sites, so we volunteered to do a survey and put in a report. At site A, we found that solid hand-soap was still being used and the cost of this must be extortionate, so we are recommending that soap dispensers be installed here; these will cost £52 each per year to rent and have serviced. We also recommend replacing the paper towels with hand-dryers, because the paper towels make the place look untidy. Hand-dryers will cost £90 per year. The number of staff at this site would necessitate two dispensers and two dryers; this number would be for each washroom, and there are four washrooms altogether on alternate floors.

We then went on to site B, a very pleasant building with excellent car-parking facilities and a good canteen. We were shown the present washroom facilities, which have both Mens and Ladies rooms on each floor; there are four floors including the ground. This site has about the same number of staff as site A, so would need the same number of soap dispensers and hand-dryers. Incidentally, we did explore the cost of buying rather than renting, but the equipment is expensive to buy and someone would need to be responsible for keeping it in order; we would probably need a service contract with a company and

Reproduced from *Developing Teams Through Project-Based Learning*,
Jean Atkinson, Gower, Aldershot, 2001.

if we had not bought the equipment from them, the servicing would be expensive.

On to site C – a very large building, with a lot more staff than either A or B. Here we were back to Mens and Ladies on alternate floors. We should need ten of each soap dispensers and hand-dryers here in each washroom – there are nine floors, with five Mens rooms and four Ladies.

Site D, which contains Head Office, is the largest building of the lot, with the senior management team being based here and having far more staff than any of the others. This is the flagship office of the company – overseas clients are all brought here – so, as you would expect, all staff facilities are excellent. The canteen here serves about ten thousand hot meals a day, as well as coffees and snacks, and when we were looking around we saw that they also use solid soap and paper towels. We realized that we really should have been including the canteens at each site in our costings, since if we are replacing equipment it would make sense to do it throughout, so we would need to add an extra soap dispenser and hand-dryer to the costings for each site, except site D, where the canteen would need two of each. At site D, there are Mens rooms on floors 1, 3, 5, 7, 9, 11 and 13 and Ladies rooms are to be found on floors 2, 4, 6, 8, 10 and 12.

All in all, we recommend acceptance of our proposals for refitting. It may be that prices would be adjusted yearly for rental, but this is something which could be looked at if these recommendations are accepted.

Your rewrite does not need to follow slavishly the example displayed on the following pages but it will give you an idea to follow and may also provide a framework for your own report.

Reproduced from *Developing Teams Through Project-Based Learning*,
Jean Atkinson, Gower, Aldershot, 2001.

REPORT AND RECOMMENDATIONS
ON POSSIBLE PROVISION
OF NEW WASHROOM EQUIPMENT
AT ALL THE COMPANY'S SITES

Report compiled
by
John Andrews and Janet Baker

Summary

Last year, the company spent a total of £5745 on soap, and £9644 on paper towels for washrooms throughout its four sites, with costs of each rising annually. Our recommendations would cost a total of £5044 for soap dispensers and £8910 for hand-dryers, with the hire cost of each fixed for four years.

Costs break down as follows:

	Last year		Recommended	
	Soap	Paper towels	Soap dispensers	Hand-dryers
Site A	£600	£920	£468	£810
Site B	£600	£920	£468	£810
Site C	£1520	£2594	£1456	£2520
Site D	£3025	£5210	£2560	£4770

There would be no installation charges for the equipment. Installation of the equipment would help with the company image in keeping the washrooms tidy.

Contents

Introduction and rationale

This project arises out of a discussion at the staff committee meeting on 12 February. The committee decided that replacement of washroom facilities at all sites should be explored. They felt that at the moment a bad image of the company is being created to visitors by the inevitable untidy disposal of paper towels in the bins, and that a lot of money must be being wasted because the cleaning staff replaced soap tablets well before they had run out. Unfortunately and surprisingly, there also seems to be some pilfering of new soap tablets. Staff at Site A volunteered to do some research into current and possible costs, and advantages and disadvantages of installing automated equipment. We allowed for a day at each site, but since this would have to be done at the same time as our current work we allowed 28 days for the whole project. We estimated that costs would be limited to working time involved and some phone calls to various sites. This would be a team project, involving the following personnel: Pauline Johnson, Janet Baker, John Andrews, Stephen Ashworth.

Methods

Pauline and John visited each site, since we thought it was important to check for ourselves the space available in each case. Janet contacted three suppliers of washroom equipment to arrange quotations and Stephen checked with the Accounts Department on last year's expenditure for each site. Having obtained price lists from each of the three companies contacted, Janet then arranged for each to do a site visit and provide a quotation.

Findings

At each site, soap tablets and paper towels were being used in all washrooms, with the inevitable untidy impression resulting, paper towels sometimes strewn around and soap-marks on washbasins. In view of the fact that a lot of outside clients visit each site, we felt that this did not convey a particularly good image of the company. Individual site details are:

Site A: Four floors, with Men's and Women's washrooms alternating on each floor – four in all. There is a small canteen on the ground floor, which also uses soap and paper towels.

Site B: Built on very much the same lines as Site C, including the needs of the canteen staff, and has washrooms also on alternating floors – four washrooms in all.

Site C: This building has nine floors, again with Men's and Women's washrooms on alternate floors plus a canteen on the first floor.

Site D: Head Office, and the Company's flagship building. Image is even more important here, since prestigious overseas clients visit regularly. The building has thirteen floors, and washroom distribution is similar to the other sites.

Recommendations

We recommend that in Sites A and B, two hand-dryers and two soap dispensers should replace the current arrangements in each washroom.

In Site C, because there are more staff, three dryers and three soap dispensers will be needed in each washroom.

At Head Office, Site D, because of the high numbers of staff, we recommend four of each piece of equipment in each washroom.

The canteens on each site should also be supplied with this equipment – one of each at each site except Site D, where our recommendation would be two of each piece of equipment.

Taking into account not only prices but also our impression of service provided, we recommend Bodgett and Runn as suppliers. They guarantee to hold all prices for four years and to clean and service all equipment bi-weekly.

Financial considerations

Site A
Two dispensers and two dryers
for each of four washrooms,
plus one of each for canteen

                               Dispensers: £468   Dryers: £810
                               (all prices p.a.)

Site B
As for Site A   Dispensers: £468   Dryers: £810

Site C
Three of each piece of equipment
for each of nine washrooms,
plus one for canteen

Dispensers: £1456   Dryers: £2520

Site D
Four pieces of equipment
for each of thirteen washrooms,
plus two for canteen

Dispensers: £2560   Dryers: £4770

Total annual cost for four-year contract: £14,862

Total current annual costs, which are likely to rise each year:
£15,389

8   So how have we developed?

The objectives of this chapter are:

1   To give ideas on conducting a post-mortem of a successful project.
2   To help you re-motivate your team after a project which was not so successful.

Your report is in, your presentation has been carried out successfully, your project is in on time, within budget, to the agreed standard. What can there possibly be left to do?

A post-mortem is a very important part of any project; it's vital in the case of yours, where you were wanting to use the learning from it to develop as a team. In fact, two post-mortems are better still – one formal, work-based one and one after work, at the nearest pub, to celebrate completion. I imagine you can organize the second without any help, so let's concentrate on the formal work-based one.

Informing personnel

It would be counter-productive to hold any kind of post-mortem with any personnel wondering what is going to happen to them next. Therefore, as soon as your project is judged satisfactory, let people know what awaits them – if you have co-opted specialist help, are the specialists now going back to their own work-place, or will you require them for your next project? Perhaps you have bought staff in on a temporary contract, maybe through an agency, for the duration of the project; let them know in plenty of time just how much longer you will require them – not simply because it's kinder, but also because you won't get the best out of people who are constantly worrying about their own futures. Remember to thank everyone, including those who will no longer be working with you; if agency staff have been with you for any length of time, it's good to give them a short written reference.

Planning through

Some time before your project was due to end, you should have 'planned through' – how are we going to capitalize on our success? Where do we go next? Although there will be a feeling of satisfaction at successful completion of the project, there may also be a slightly flat feeling – a feeling of 'what now?' It was stressful at times, but it's left a hole now – a bit like having an aching tooth out. Be ready for this, and be ready to discuss what's next. Some time before your project was due to end, you should have 'planned through' – how are we going to capitalize on our success? Where do we go next? This planning through is very important. A few years ago, I was doing a lengthy management training assignment with a company in Hertfordshire. The local football team, to most people's surprise, had had a giant-killing season, and reached the Cup Final, playing against one of the very top teams in the then Division One. I am not a football fan, but knowing that on the Monday all the talk in the company would be about what had happened at Wembley on the Saturday, I decided to watch for the sake of my credibility. In fact, from a management point of view, it was very interesting. Almost from the kick-off, it became obvious that the local team's objective had been to get to Wembley – and they'd done it. The more experienced team had planned through: 'we're going to get to Wembley – and then we're going to win the Cup and then [I strongly suspect] start training to do it all over again next year'. They won.

You need, then, to be ready to discuss with your team what's coming next. I don't mean to suggest that you start another project immediately; you can't keep climbing for ever, and you all need a chance to get your breath back. It would be a pity, though, to lose all the impetus for teamwork that has been created. Have some questions ready for discussion at the post-mortem meeting, having given some thought to them yourself beforehand. You'll probably get more response if you ask them to discuss the questions in pairs or trios:

- What were our successes? What can we be proud of?
- If we were asked to carry out a similar project now, what we would do differently?
- How much of our success is due to our own efforts?
- Is there anything about our performance that we're disappointed with? To what extent were we responsible? How could we avoid this another time? To what extent were outside factors responsible? Could we plan for risk of these another time?
- What have we learned about ways of working – have we learned a better or quicker way to do tasks which we did on a regular basis before?
- Have we had any surprise about the company and how it works?
- What skills do we believe we now have amongst us which we did not have before this project?
- Do you think we are stronger as a team than we were at the beginning of the project? Can you give specific examples?
- What have we learned about working together? How can we carry forward the lessons we've learned about ourselves as a team? Are there particular occasions when this needs to happen?

- Is there anything we still need to work on to improve the way we work together?

And suppose – Heaven forbid! – that your project hasn't been a resounding success? Perhaps it never really recovered from slippage at the beginning, or you seriously underestimated the costs involved, so that the quality of the 'finished product', whether tangible or intangible, is not what you hoped. Then it's even more important to ask these same questions, above all, 'What have we learnt?' It may well be that you have learned that the idea is impossible to put into practice, or that no one can produce that many widgets in that space of time for that amount of money. This is perfectly valid learning, and (I'm sorry to sound like Pollyanna, but I believe this very strongly) if you can view any failure as a learning experience, then that experience is worthwhile. Don't allow negative talk and breast-beating at your post-mortem meeting – in fact it's probably better to call it a review meeting if it has not been successful; post-mortem underlines the fact that it's dead.

I hope, though, that your project has been a success and that your team is ready for further challenges. Off to the pub! Congratulations – and good luck with the next project!

Sheets one, two and three are for you to photocopy to use at your post-mortem meeting.

Sheet one

Successes from this project are:

We achieved these successes by:

We can build on our success factors by:

Sheet two

If we were starting again, we should do differently:

We were disappointed in our performance in:

Next time, we should have to build into our risk assessment:

Sheet three

Our teamwork has been positively affected by:

We still need to work on this aspect of teamwork:

We shall do this by:

We shall particularly need teamwork when:

Skills mix

This sheet is for you to use in your own review of the project, and to compare with the Skills Mix sheet in Chapter 1.

Following completion of the project, we now have more:

People who analyse objectively
People who are strong on meeting deadlines
People who are good communicators
People who are good at administration
'Ideas' people
People who work well with other people
Good listeners
People who can do as they are told

Because of this, I can now delegate more ....
work to ....

Appendix A: Suggested projects

It may be that you would like to use project-based learning to develop your team, but are deterred by the thought of the time and expense involved in setting up a project. In fact, a worthwhile project can be set up for very little outlay indeed – take, for instance, the project we discussed throughout Chapters 3 and 4 in this book, improving customer service by telephone. There is very little cost involved, at least to do the research, and if it is used as a team exercise, then no one individual is going to spend a lot of time on it. In the rest of this chapter, you will find suggestions for various projects which also cost very little in time or money, but will help you achieve your objective. I have provided a blank Gantt chart which can be photocopied for each project, though it is course impossible to provide critical path analyses since these will differ with each project. I hope very much that even if none of these is appropriate for you in the form in which they are set out here, they will act as springboards for adaptation.

You might find it a useful exercise either for yourself or for your team, if you are new to project management, to complete a Gantt chart for each project, even if at this stage the project itself would not be an appropriate one for your team.

143

Project 1

Objective

To improve the way our team works together by instigating an efficient method of ensuring that telephone calls are passed on to the appropriate person for action.

Activities and tasks

- Identify how many times in the past six months breakdown has occurred between a telephone message being taken and its being received by the person for whom it was intended.
- Brainstorm for ideas on improvement.
- Explore any recording methods which might help the situation.
- Identify where the breakdown is occurring.
- Instigate new agreed method of improvement.
- After an agreed trial period, review to see how well the project is working.
- Decide on any necessary changes to agreed methods.

Project 2

Objective

To improve working together with the accounts team by identifying why so many customers are taking longer and longer to pay bills.

Activities and tasks

- Get co-operation from the Accounts department.
- Obtain a list of slow-payers from Accounts.
- Divide list between our own team members.
- Train staff on the approach to take.
- Decide how many people each can expect to contact in a day, given that everyone has regular work to do.
- Devise record forms for customers' answers.

Activity	Start date	End date	Duration	Time-scale

Figure A.1 Blank Gantt chart

- Identify whether any change in procedures is necessary from any department to encourage customers to speed up payment.
- Present ideas to the departments concerned.

Project 3

Objective
To improve teamwork in our own team by introducing training on working together.

Activities and tasks

- Discuss with team examples of the ways in which our working together is currently not as good as we would wish.
- Discuss the answer to: 'How will we know when our working together is satisfactory?'
- Identify six training organizations which offer suitable programmes, and obtain their brochures.
- Identify any team leader within our own organization who might be able to provide us with necessary training in-house.
- Decide on suitable trainer.
- Arrange dates.
- Brief team members.
- Training takes place.
- Debrief team members and agree action points.

Project 4

Objective
To explore flexi-time as a way of improving staff recruitment, retention and motivation.

Activities and tasks

- Identify busiest times, when core-time would have to operate.

- Examine records of leaving interviews over the past two years, to see how many cite hours as a reason for leaving.
- Design questionnaires for all staff to get their reaction to the proposal.
- Collate and examine results of questionnaire.
- Decide on flexi-time parameters and working.
- Nominate one department as a pilot.
- Instigate flexi-working in this department for three months.
- Identify any areas for change.
- Roll out flexi-working throughout the company.

Project 5

Objective
To improve staff relations throughout the company by cutting down lunchtime queues in the canteen.

Activities and tasks

- Talk to catering staff to ascertain how other departments could make their life easier.
- Identify why so many people go to lunch at the same time.
- Meet with other departmental managers to ascertain whether staggering of lunch-hours would be possible.
- Explore how each department could help to provide cover for another if necessary.
- Implement procedures.
- Arrange a date to review success.

Project 6

Objective
To improve relationships with end-users in other departments by cutting preparation time for production of requested computer programs.

Activities and tasks

- Identify how many complaints we currently receive about time taken.
- Identify from where these complaints come.
- Identify how much delay is accountable to ourselves, and how much is caused by the end-users themselves.
- Meet with all end-users in turn to discuss acceptable turnaround times from receiving request to delivery.
- Identify any particularly busy periods.
- Discuss how end-users can help us speed things up.
- Agree procedures for informing end-users if unforeseen delays are likely.
- Implement agreed procedures for speeding up.
- Set a review date.

Appendix B: Further reading

Here are some books on topics we have covered

For understanding more about yourself and other people
Harris, T. (1967), *I'm OK, You're OK*, London: Pan.
Cary Cooper and Peter Makin (1981), *Psychology for Managers*, British Psychological Society.
Ian Stewart and Van Joines (1987), *TA Today*, Lifespace.
Rupert Brown (1988), *Group Processes*, London: Blackwell.

For understanding personalities
Isabel Briggs and Peter Myers (1980), *Gifts Differing*, Consulting Psychologists Press.
Gordon Lawrence (1979), *People Types & Tiger Stripes*, Centre for Applications of Psychological Type.

For handling conflict
Edward de Bono (1985), *Conflicts*, Harmondsworth: Pelican Books.
Edward de Bono (1971), *Lateral Thinking for Management*, Harmondsworth: Pelican Books.
Edward de Bono (1991), *I am Right – You are Wrong*, Harmondsworth: Penguin Books.

For handling stress
Jacqueline Atkinson (1994), *Coping with Stress at Work*, Thorsen.

For improving communication
Robert Thoules (1956), *Straight & Crooked Thinking*, London: Pan.
Eric Berne (1974), *What Do You Say After You Say Hello?*, London: Corgi.
Eric Berne (1964), *Games People Play*, Harmondsworth: Penguin Books.
Ken and Kater Back (1982), *Assertiveness at Work*, Guild.
Julian Fast (1980), *Body Language*, Tower.

For motivating your team
Mark McCormack (1983), *The 110% Solution*, London: Pan.

For motivating yourself
Wayne Dyer (1977), *Your Erroneous Zones*, London: Sphere.
Wayne Dyer (1989), *You'll See It When You Believe It*, Schwarz.

For selling your ideas to other people
Jean Atkinson (1998), *Teach Yourself Selling*, London: Hodder Headline.

Index

Gower Handbook of Training and Development

Third Edition

Edited by Anthony Landale

It is now crystal clear that, in today's ever-changing world, an organization's very survival depends upon how it supports its people to learn and keep on learning. Of course this new imperative has considerable implications for trainers who are now playing an increasingly critical role in supporting individuals, teams and business management. In this respect today's trainers may need to be more than excellent presenters; they are also likely to require a range of consultancy and coaching skills, to understand the place of technology in supporting learning and be able to align personal development values with business objectives.

This brand new edition of the *Gower Handbook of Training and Development* will be an invaluable aid for today's training professional as they face up to the organizational challenges presented to them. All 38 chapters in this edition are new and many of the contributors, whilst being best-selling authors or established industry figures, are appearing for the first time in this form. Edited by Anthony Landale, this *Handbook* builds on the foundations that previous editions have laid down whilst, at the same time, highlighting many of the very latest advances in the industry.

The *Handbook* is divided into five sections - learning organization, best practice, advanced techniques in training and development, the use of IT in learning, and evaluation issues.

Gower

Handling Groups in Action

The Use of Distinctions in Facilitation

Dale Hunter, Anne Bailey and Bill Taylor

What do you do when the group you are facilitating gets stuck, caught in a loop covering the same old ground, is unable to agree on anything, is working too slowly, is unfocused, or encounters one of the many problems that can get in the way of reaching a conclusion?

This book by the authors of *The Facilitation of Groups* presents a fresh approach for the experienced facilitator. It focuses on the key skill of noticing what is missing in a group's interaction and finding a way of introducing the missing elements or 'distinctions' while the group is in action. It explores a number of these distinctions including:

- purpose and culture
- powerful listening and speaking
- fearlessness and ruthless compassion
- intuition
- affirmation and celebration
- safety and trust
- intentionality
- emotional competence
- completion

and offers ways to generate them. Each distinction is described and then suggestions and processes are given to help generate it in the group.

Gower

Team-Based Learning

Howard Hills

There are two skills or competencies that appear almost without fail in every organization's 'wish-list' for the next decade: the ability to work well within a team and the ability to learn. But what if the two concepts are effectively synonymous?

Howard Hills' *Team-Based Learning* shows how the ability to learn lies at the heart of effective working in teams. His book identifies the ingredients that turn good teams into teams that improve.

These ingredients include established models of learning, of individual personality and of organizational culture, as well as some models of his own. He provides a picture of what team-based learning looks like and explains how our understanding of the ways in which individuals learn; how teams form, build and develop; and how the effect of personality on both processes can provide us with the raw materials for managing the process.

Team-Based Learning includes the tools for managing the process, the skills of learning and communicating within the team. It also provides a strategy for everyone involved in the process:

- the team leader, whose behaviour has such a great influence on team culture and performance;
- the team member, who needs to understand how he/she can affect the process and needs the motivation to become involved; and
- the training department, who need to create a climate in which team-based learning can flourish.

Howard Hills has written a convincing and authoritative book that will help trainers and line-managers understand the process of team-based learning; view it in the context of team roles, personality types and organizational culture; and move it from their 'wish-list' to their 'to-do' list.

Gower